THE ULTIMATE END-OF-LIFE PLANNING GUIDE

Relieve Family Burden, Avoid Conflict, and Ensure Your Wishes Are Honored After You Are Gone

Nicole Reap

© Copyright 2025 Nicole Reap - All rights reserved.

The content contained within this book may not be reproduced, duplicated, or transmitted without direct written permission from the author or the publisher.

Under no circumstances will any blame or legal responsibility be held against the publisher, or author, for any damages, reparation, or monetary loss due to the information contained within this book. Either directly or indirectly. You are responsible for your own choices, actions, and results.

Legal Notice:

This book is copyright protected. This book is only for personal use. You cannot amend, distribute, sell, use, quote, or paraphrase any part of the content within this book without the consent of the author or publisher.

Disclaimer Notice:

Please note that the information contained within this document is for educational and entertainment purposes only. All effort has been executed to present accurate, up-to-date, reliable, and complete information. No warranties of any kind are declared or implied. Readers acknowledge that the author is not engaging in the rendering of legal, financial, medical, or professional advice. The content within this book has been derived from various sources. Please consult a licensed professional before attempting any techniques outlined in this book.

By reading this document, the reader agrees that under no circumstances is the author responsible for any losses, direct or indirect, which are incurred as a result of the use of the information contained within this document, including, but not limited to, — errors, omissions, or inaccuracies.

Contents

Acknowledgements	VII
Foreword	IX
Introduction	XI
1. Setting the Stage for Peace	1

    Why Planning Is the Best Gift You Can Give
    Humor in Planning: Lightening the Load
    Finding Your Motivation: Protecting Family Harmony
    Gathering Your Essential Supplies and Mindset
    The Art of Communication: Talking to Your Family About Your Plans

2. Personal Information Essentials	11

    Who Are You? Documenting Personal Identification
    Beyond the Basics: Including Your Unique Identifiers
    Mapping Family Connections: Creating a Family Tree
    Emergency Contacts: Who to Call When You're Not There

3. Financial Affairs Simplified	19

    Banking on Simplicity: Listing Your Accounts
    Investments and Portfolios: Making Sense of Your Assets
    Insurance Policies: Securing the Future
    Comprehensive Insurance Checklist

    Debt and Obligations: Acknowledging Financial Responsibilities

    Putting It All Together: Creating a Financial Snapshot

4. Digital Legacy Management   31

    Passwords and Profiles: Keeping Digital Access Secure

    Social Media Afterlife: Handling Online Presences

    Digital Vaults: Storing and Sharing Vital Information

5. Healthcare Wishes and Legal Preparations   41

    Power of Attorney: Who Will Speak for You?

    Living Wills: Your Voice When You Can't Speak

    Understanding Advance Directives: Making Informed Choices

    Legal Contacts: Building Your Support Team

6. Funeral and Burial Plans   51

    Final Wishes: Funeral and Burial Preferences

    Cremation vs. Burial: Weighing Your Options

    Personalizing the Ceremony: Reflecting Your Life

    Writing Your Obituary: It's Your Story to Tell

7. Property and Real Estate   61

    Home Sweet Home: Documenting Real Estate

    Deeds and Titles: Understanding Ownership

    Valuing Your Assets: Real Estate Appraisals

    Sharing and Inheriting Property: Avoiding Family Feuds

8. Legacy and Personal Messages   71

    Words to Remember: Crafting Personal Messages

    Lasting Legacies: Passing on Values and Traditions

    Nature's Legacy: Our Family Cookbook

    Family Heirlooms: Deciding Who Gets Grandma's Vase

    Letters to Loved Ones: Your Final Goodbyes

9. Organizing and Storing Your Planner — 81
    Paper vs. Digital: Deciding the Best Format
    Sharing the Key: Who Needs Access?
    Regular Updates: Keeping Your Planner Current

10. Ensuring Implementation and Family Engagement — 91
    Family Meetings: Sharing Your Plans
    Handling Resistance: When Family Disagrees
    Bridging the Generation Gap: Engaging Younger Family Members
    Reviewing and Revising: Keeping Your Plans Relevant
    Legal Review: Ensuring Compliance
    Feedback and Improvement: Learning from Your Family's Input
    Celebrating Life: Planning a Living Memorial
    Finding Peace: Letting Go and Moving On

Conclusion — 107
Glossary — 111
About the Author — 115
References — 117

Acknowledgements

Writing this book has been an incredible journey, and I am profoundly grateful to the amazing individuals who made it possible. Your support, expertise, and encouragement have been invaluable, and this book is as much a reflection of your contributions as it is my vision.

To Neil Tyra, thank you for writing the foreword and for your wise counsel and advice throughout this process. Your guidance and perspective have been invaluable, and your words set the perfect tone for this book.

To Nature Wolfson, my sister-in-law, thank you for sharing your inspiration to create a family cookbook. Your creativity and passion for preserving family traditions sparked ideas that have deeply influenced my work.

To David and Laura McCutcheon, thank you for sharing the heartfelt story of your mother and how she planned her funeral. Your openness and willingness to share such a personal experience added a meaningful and inspiring perspective to this book.

To Nancy Mitchell and Sharron Mann, thank you for sharing the stories of how your mothers planned their end-of-life celebrations. Your reflections on their thoughtful preparations and the impact it had on your families brought depth and humanity to this project.

To my girls, Rachel and Madison, thank you for your endless encouragement. Your belief in me has been the foundation of my perseverance and inspiration. You are the reason that I continue to grow and learn.

To Lynette Stewart, editor, thank you for your meticulous feedback and dedication to refining my work. Your attention to detail and thoughtful suggestions made this book so much stronger.

Finally, to my readers, thank you for trusting me to be part of your journey. I hope this book brings value, inspiration, and empowerment to your life.

This book is a testament to collaboration, learning, and shared passion. Thank you all for being part of this incredible experience.

Foreword

When I first came across this manuscript, *The Ultimate End-of-Life Planning Guide,* my immediate reaction was, "This is the book I wish I had written for my clients." As a licensed trust and estates attorney in Maryland, I spend my days helping people navigate the complex, often overwhelming world of estate planning. Drafting wills, creating trusts, and establishing powers of attorney are all vital pieces of the puzzle. But they're just that—pieces. The bigger picture is often missing: the practical, human side of planning that ensures your family can carry out your wishes with clarity and confidence. That's where this book comes in, and Nicole Reap has done a magnificent job.

This isn't a legal guide, nor does it claim to be. Instead, it's the perfect companion to the legal advice you'll receive from an attorney. It's packed with practical tips, insightful advice, and a few laugh-out-loud moments. The author, a local educator with a knack for breaking down complicated topics, has created a roadmap for the part of end-of-life planning that too often gets overlooked: the day-to-day details that your loved ones will need to manage after you're gone.

Here's the thing: as attorneys, we can craft the most airtight legal documents imaginable, but we can't answer questions like, "Who should I call first if something happens?" or, "Where does Mom keep the deed to the house?" This book bridges that gap beautifully. It's the step-by-step guide your family needs to ensure that your wishes are honored and your legacy is preserved without unnecessary stress, confusion, or family drama.

I particularly love how this book takes what could be a somber topic and makes it approachable—even fun. The checklists, quizzes, and humor sprinkled throughout make what could feel like a chore into something empowering. And let's face it, planning for the inevitable is one of the most loving, responsible things you can do for the people you care about most.

Moreover, this book doesn't just focus on the practical but also embraces the profoundly personal. From writing letters to your loved ones to organizing a funeral that reflects your personality and values, the author shows you how to leave behind more than just legal documents. You'll leave behind clarity, comfort, and even a few smiles during a tough time.

So, whether you're just starting to think about end-of-life planning or have already worked with an attorney to establish the legal framework, this guide will fill the gaps and bring everything together. It's a book that makes planning easier and gives you peace of mind, knowing you've done everything you can to protect and support your family.

To anyone reading this: Don't just skim the pages. Dive in, use the checklists, reflect on the questions, and take action. You'll give your loved ones one of the greatest gifts imaginable—a clear plan, a steady hand, and the assurance that you've got their back even after you're gone.

Neil W. Tyra, Esq.
The Tyra Law Firm, LLC
(301)315-0811
neiltyra@tyralawfirm.com
www.tyralawfirm.com
www.linkedin.com/in/tyralawfirm

Introduction

When my mother passed away suddenly while I was in college, our family was thrown into a whirlwind of grief and unanticipated decisions. My younger brother was just sixteen, and my sister was only nine. In the chaos that followed, we had no say in what happened to my mother's personal items—her clothing, shoes, jewelry, or other keepsakes. There was no plan or list of wishes for her belongings. My father did what he felt was best, donating most of her clothing and shoes and selling her jewelry to cover our immediate needs. Looking back now, I wish I had asked to keep a few precious items, simple tokens that might have helped me feel closer to her, to remember her beautiful soul and the vibrant woman she had been.

Years later, we faced similar heartache when my grandfather passed away. He hadn't made any plans for my grandmother's financial security or laid out a clear path for how she would manage without him. The responsibility of her care fell to my father and his brother, but the strain of this responsibility took a toll on their relationship. They were forced into financial decisions neither of them had been prepared for, and before long, misunderstandings and resentments began to surface. Eventually, my uncle estranged himself from our family. When my grandmother passed, we found out only weeks later through a cousin, as my uncle hadn't informed us or any of my grandmother's extended family. My siblings, my father, and I missed our mother and grandmother's funeral, so we ended up organizing a small memorial service of our own to find closure and grieve her loss.

I understand that not every family experiences what mine did, but I'm sharing this story to highlight the importance of planning for the future. Losing a loved one is already painful, and uncertainty around their belongings, finances, or final wishes can make that loss even harder to bear. Through this book, I hope to guide you in preparing thoughtfully so that your loved ones can honor you in the way you would want, without the added stress of unresolved decisions. Taking the time now to organize your affairs is a true act of love—a gift that spares those you care about from confusion and offers them peace.

So, what's the purpose of this book? Consider it a library of resources designed to relieve family burdens, dodge conflicts, and ensure your wishes are honored- just as the subtitle says. We will discuss estate planning, living wills, Power of Attorney, insurance policies, medical advance directives, and more. But here's the twist—the book is sprinkled with humor. Let's face it, the topic of death doesn't usually come with a side of laughs. We're here to change that. By adding a dash of levity, we make the subject approachable and manageable without meaning any disrespect.

Who's this book for? The answer is simple: it's for anyone who's ever considered the future—whether you're a seasoned estate planner or someone who's never thought beyond next week's grocery list. If you're an adult looking to organize your affairs responsibly, you've come to the right place. This book speaks to both the experienced planner and the novice, ensuring everyone finds value in its pages.

Now, let's talk structure. This book isn't just a series of dry instructions—it's an interactive guide full of checklists, quizzes, and engaging sections designed to make you think. You'll find plenty of helpful resources pointing you to useful websites and apps. It's designed to support you every step of the way, making the planning process as straightforward as possible. And here's the best part: I've created a digital workbook for you to use alongside this book. This workbook is a companion designed to keep you organized and focused while you work through each chapter. While many planners stick to the logistics, this one adds a personal touch to make the journey enjoyable—rather than overwhelming. It's a unique blend of practicality and wit, ensuring that you'll make progress and have a little fun along the way, too!

Call to Action:

Scan this QR Code to Receive Your Workbook and Planner!

End of Life Planner

Here's another **call to action**: Get stuck in, engage with the content, and see the benefits for yourself. Completing this planner will help you achieve peace of mind and will nurture harmony among your loved ones. With every section you complete, you're taking a step towards ensuring that your wishes are clear and your family is spared unnecessary stress.

Let me end on a personal note. As you begin this book, take a moment to reflect on your motivations. Consider the impact your planning efforts will have on those you care about. This book is a helping hand from me to you, aimed at making a challenging topic just a little bit easier to handle. Let's take a quick quiz to see how prepared you are right now.

Welcome to the "Plan for the Inevitable" quiz!

Take a few minutes to assess how well you've prepared for the end-of-life planning process. Don't worry, there are no wrong answers—just a few things to think about as you begin planning.

1. Have you written a will or trust?
   A. Yes, and I review it every year to make sure it's up to date.
   B. I have one, but it's been a while since I checked on it.
   C. No, I haven't written one yet.

2. Do you have a Power of Attorney (POA) for financial and medical decisions
   A. Absolutely—I've chosen a trusted person for both, and we've discussed it.
   B. I have one for financial decisions, but I need to set up one for medical decisions.
   C. Nope, I haven't appointed anyone yet.

3. How clear are your wishes for medical treatment if you can't make decisions for yourself?
   A. I've filled out an advanced health directive and discussed it with my family.
   B. I've thought about it, but I haven't put anything in writing yet
   C. I haven't really thought about it.

4. Do you have any "digital assets" (social media, online accounts, or digital subscriptions) you want to be managed after you're gone?
   A. Yes, I've already set up digital executors for my accounts.
   B. I've thought about it but haven't taken any action yet.
   C. No, but maybe I should.

5. Do you talk openly with your family about your after-death plans?
   A. Yes, we've had honest conversations, and everyone knows my wishes.
   B. We've talked a little, but I could probably be more detailed.
   C. I've never really discussed it with anyone.

6. Do you have any important documents (like life insurance, bank accounts, or property titles) that your loved ones know how to access?
   A. Yes, everything's organized and easily accessible.
   B. I have some, but I should probably make things more accessible.
   C. Not really—they wouldn't have a clue where to find everything.

7. Have you considered leaving a personal letter or message for your loved ones to guide them?
   A. Yes, I've written letters and recorded messages for special occasions.
   B. I've thought about it but haven't written anything yet.
   C. No, I haven't considered that.

8. How confident are you in your financial and estate planning?
   A. Very confident—everything is in order and planned out.
   B. I'm on the right track, but I could use a bit more guidance.
   C. Not confident at all—I haven't started any real planning.

Scoring:

Count your answers and see where you stand!

- Mostly A's: You're a planning pro! You're well ahead of the curve and well-prepared for the future. Keep up the good work, but remember to revisit these plans every so often to keep them up to date. However, keep reading because you will find more up-to-date information

- Mostly B's: You're on the right track! You've made some important decisions, but there's still room for a little more organization and clarity. This guide will help fill in the gaps.

- Mostly C's: It's time to start planning! Don't worry, it's never too late to begin organizing your affairs. This guide will help you take your first steps toward a secure future for you and your loved ones.

Chapter 1

SETTING THE STAGE FOR PEACE

The other day, I stumbled across a headline that read, "Man Leaves Entire Inheritance to Pet Parrot, Family Furious." It was one of those stories that seemed too crazy to be true, yet it perfectly encapsulates the chaos that can unfold without proper planning. The heart of the matter isn't about the pet parrot—although Polly certainly won the lottery—but about the unexpected twists and turns when we leave our affairs to chance. While the story might seem absurd, it serves as a humorous yet poignant reminder of why we should get ahead of these matters while we can. Planning for the inevitable isn't about inviting gloom; rather, it's about setting the stage for peace, clarity, and a smoother transition for the loved ones we leave behind.

Why Planning Is the Best Gift You Can Give

You might be wondering why planning is such a significant gift. By taking the time to outline your final wishes, you're giving your family the ultimate present: peace of mind. Think about it—when the time comes, your family will already be grappling with the emotional weight of loss. Your foresight can spare them the added burden of piecing together your affairs, trying to guess what you might have wanted, or worse, facing disagreements over assets and decisions. By clearly documenting your wishes, you're offering them a roadmap that guides them through one of life's most challenging times. It's like leaving behind a comforting whisper that says, "I've got this covered. Just follow my lead."

Beyond the practicalities, planning delivers profound emotional benefits. There's a distinct sense of completion in knowing that your affairs are in order. It's empowering to take charge of your destiny, even when it pertains to events that unfold in your absence. This control provides comfort and closure, allowing you to focus on living your life to the fullest, without the nagging worry of what might happen if you're not around to steer the ship. It's the peace of mind that comes from knowing you've done everything possible to ease the path for those you leave behind.

Practically speaking, organizing your affairs in advance streamlines the entire process for executors and heirs. When your estate is neatly tied up with clear instructions, it simplifies the management of assets and the navigation of legal hurdles. Executors aren't left scrambling to gather documents or decipher cryptic hints about your intentions. Instead, they can focus on honoring your wishes efficiently, ensuring that everything unfolds as smoothly as possible. This efficiency saves time and energy and minimizes the potential for missteps or misunderstandings.

Of course, discussing these topics with a bit of humor can make the entire endeavor less daunting. While doing research for this book, I came upon a story about a man who left a note in his will, reading, "Bury me with my favorite golf clubs—just in case they have a course in heaven." It's that kind of lightheartedness that can ease the discomfort of these conversations, making them more approachable and less intimidating. We can use humor to open the door to deeper discussions, allowing us to tackle the task with a smile instead of a frown.

> **Call to Action: Thoughts for Loved Ones**
> Take a moment to think about your wishes. What small steps can you take today to start this process? Write down three things you want your loved ones to know or do when you're no longer here. This is your starting point—a gentle nudge to begin setting the stage for peace. For example, my mother and her cousin promised each other that if something happened to one of them, the other would keep the family together and make sure the children stayed in touch with one another.

As you read further, remember that planning is an act of love. It's a thoughtful gesture that transcends time, ensuring that your legacy is one of care, consideration, and a touch of humor. Whether it's a note about golf clubs or a detailed plan for your assets, each step you take today is a gift to those you cherish.

Humor in Planning: Lightening the Load

While talking about what happens after we pass away isn't typically a laughing matter, humor can be the secret ingredient that transforms a somber topic into something a bit more approachable. By injecting a little levity, we open up the dialogue, making it easier for everyone involved. For instance, you could gather the family together and break the ice with a light-hearted quip: "I'm not planning on kicking the bucket anytime soon, but I figured it's time to get my ducks in a row." It's these moments of humor that can make a potentially awkward conversation feel more like a casual chat over Sunday brunch. The ability to laugh in the face of life's final inevitability helps to diffuse tension, allowing us to discuss serious matters without feeling overwhelmed.

Humor can also find its place in the planning itself. Consider the idea of a punny epitaph—something like "Finally Finished My To-Do List" or "I Told You I Was Sick." These playful touches can bring a smile to loved ones' faces when they need it most. Including witty clauses in a will can have a similar effect. One might specify, tongue-in-cheek, that their ashes be scattered over their favorite beach, "but only on sunny days, and preferably not during tourist season." These elements of humor lighten the mood and make the planning process more personal and memorable. Remember, the goal isn't to make light of the situation but to bring a sense of joy and humanity to it.

It's important to tread carefully when using humor in planning. What one person finds hilarious, another might find offensive. This is where cultural sensitivity and respect come into play. We must consider our audience and choose our words carefully. Humor should never belittle or undermine the gravity of the situation but instead, offer a moment of relief. Balancing humor with respect ensures that it complements the discussion rather than detracts from it. Think of it as seasoning—the right amount can enhance the flavor, but too much can overpower the dish.

Personal anecdotes are another way to weave humor into planning. Sharing a funny family story or cherished memory can make the process feel less clinical and more heartfelt. Perhaps there's a running joke in the family about Uncle Joe's legendary snoring or Grandma's habit of hiding candy in the oddest places. These stories can be included in personal letters or as part of a farewell speech. By incorporating these personal touches, we remind our loved ones of the joy and laughter we've shared, creating a legacy that celebrates a life well-lived.

> **Call to Action: Memories**
> Reflect on a humorous memory you've shared with your family. Write it down and consider how you might include it in your planning. This doesn't have to be a grand gesture—perhaps it's a simple note in your will or a story to be shared at a future gathering. By doing so, you're planning for the future and creating a moment that will keep your memory alive in the most light-hearted way at the same time.

Finding Your Motivation: Protecting Family Harmony

Some family gatherings turn ugly when, for instance, a heated debate erupts over who gets Aunt Joan's heirloom clock. It's a scene that plays out more often than we'd like to admit and one that can be avoided with thoughtful planning. Family harmony should be a driving force behind every decision you make in your after-death planning. By taking the time to articulate your wishes, you can prevent common disputes that arise over assets or cherished items. You have the power to maintain unity even when you're not there, ensuring that your family remains a close-knit unit. This will avoid arguments and preserve the love and respect that define your family relationships.

Beyond the immediate family dynamics, planning provides an opportunity to reflect on your motivations. Think about the legacy you want to leave behind. Is it one of generosity, wisdom, or resilience? Your motivations might stem from a desire to ensure your wishes are respected or from a need to make things easier for those you love. These personal aspirations shape the decisions you make, guiding you in crafting a legacy that aligns with your values and beliefs. You can take control of the narrative you leave, making sure it reflects who you are and what you stand for. In doing so, you help your family approach the future with clarity and purpose.

Family dynamics can be as complex as they are varied. Blended families, estranged relationships, and different cultural expectations can all contribute to the intricacies of planning. Blended families, in particular, may face unique challenges when it comes to inheritance and decision-making. By addressing these complexities head-on, you can create a plan that accounts for everyone's needs and expectations. This might involve developing strategies to bridge gaps between estranged family members or finding ways to honor the diverse traditions within your family. Recognize the potential hurdles and work proactively to overcome them, ensuring that your plan is inclusive and considerate of all involved.

To start this process with family harmony in mind, you could arrange regular family meetings. These gatherings offer a platform for open discussions, allowing everyone to voice their thoughts and concerns. They provide an opportunity to share your plans and gather feedback, making adjustments as needed to ensure everyone feels heard and valued. A family communication plan can also be instrumental in keeping everyone on the same page. This might include setting up group emails, creating a shared calendar for important dates, or designating a family liaison to coordinate updates. These actionable steps lay the groundwork for a harmonious future, promoting understanding and cooperation among family members.

In the end, finding your motivation for planning should come from leaving a legacy of love and unity. You want to ensure your family can move forward together, hand in hand, without the shadow of disputes or uncertainties. By focusing on family harmony, you'll protect your loved ones from potential conflicts and provide a foundation of connection and support that will endure through the years.

Gathering Your Essential Supplies and Mindset

Taking on the task of after-death planning requires more than just a willing heart; it demands careful preparation. This preparation involves both practical and intangible resources, each helping to ensure your efforts are thorough and effective.

First, let's talk about the essentials you'll need. Notebooks and planners are helpful in this process. A durable, easy-to-handle notebook is great for jotting down thoughts, making lists, and organizing plans. It's your personal space to capture ideas whenever they arise and bring order to the complexities of planning. Planners, on the other hand, help you structure your tasks, set deadlines, and stay organized, ensuring that nothing is overlooked.

In our digital age, there's also a place for technology for these tasks. Digital organization apps come in handy for those who prefer a tech-savvy approach. Applications like Evernote or Trello allow you to create digital lists, set reminders, and store important documents, all within the reach of your smartphone or computer. These digital tools can sync across devices, offering convenience and accessibility wherever you are. They're particularly useful for those who juggle multiple responsibilities, allowing you to manage your planning on the go.

Let's not forget about legal resources and documents, which form the backbone of any effective plan. This includes wills, advance directives, and power of attorney forms—documents that ensure your wishes are legally recognized and respected. You must have these documents in place as they provide clarity and prevent potential legal entanglements for your loved ones.

For those seeking additional guidance, numerous resources are available. Numerous websites and apps offer a wealth of information and support, catering to various aspects of planning. U.S. Bank's estate planning guide offers practical advice and resources. Apps designed for digital organization, like Final Security, help manage digital assets, ensuring that your online presence is accounted for in your planning. These resources serve as valuable companions, offering guidance and support as you plan.

The Art of Communication: Talking to Your Family About Your Plans

Communication is the secret sauce of after-death planning—without it, your grand plans might end up looking more like a game of telephone than a smooth transition. At its core, it ensures your wishes are respected and your legacy doesn't accidentally get hijacked by your great aunt's obsession with "repainting the family portrait." Having open conversations with family members is firstly just good manners. It's also a must if you want your plans understood and followed, rather than misinterpreted into something...let's say, less than you intended. You want to set the stage for a flawless execution of your wishes, with no surprise plot twists. When everyone's on the same page, the chance of misunderstandings drops from "catastrophic" to "almost impossible." Clear communication helps us get through those tricky, sensitive topics and creates a trust-filled environment where your family isn't guessing whether you meant to leave them your antique spoon collection or donate it to a museum. In short, it's about painting a crystal-clear picture of your desires so there's no room for, "Wait, she wanted me to do *what* with her stuff?"

Starting these conversations can feel daunting, but you must approach them with intention and sensitivity. Timing and setting are important for how the dialogue unfolds. Perhaps you could broach the subject during a family gathering when everyone is relaxed and receptive, maybe over a shared meal or a casual Sunday afternoon. You don't want to drop a bombshell but rather ease into the discussion with gentle prompts. You might say, "I've been thinking about getting my affairs in order, and I'd love to hear your thoughts." These conversation starters invite participation without overwhelming your audience. They signal your openness to feedback and discussion, setting a collaborative tone for the conversation.

Yet, despite your best efforts, resistance might arise. It's natural for some family members to feel uncomfortable or even dismissive when confronted with the realities of after-death planning. Acknowledge these feelings without dismissing them, and remind yourself that patience is a virtue here. Address resistance with empathy, perhaps by sharing your motivations for planning. Explain that your goal is to alleviate stress, not add to it. Overcoming awkwardness requires a delicate balance of honesty and tact. Be prepared for some initial discomfort, and understand that persistence and kindness often pave the way to acceptance.

Once the initial conversations are underway, maintaining momentum becomes essential. Regular updates provide a platform for ongoing dialogue, keeping everyone informed as your plans evolve. You could schedule periodic family meetings or set up a group chat for easy communication. This will ensure that updates are shared consistently, preventing any surprises or last-minute changes. Involving family in the planning process encourages collaboration and reinforces the importance of unity and shared responsibility. It transforms planning into a collective endeavor, where everyone has a voice and a stake in the outcome.

Ultimately, the goal of these conversations is to generate mutual respect and understanding. Your goal is to ensure your family feels included and valued, not sidelined or overlooked. Effective communication holds the planning process together, bridging gaps and building connections. By prioritizing open dialogue, you lay the groundwork for a future where your wishes are honored and celebrated. You create a legacy of clarity and consideration, one that resonates with those you hold dear.

As we wrap up this chapter on planning, take a moment to pause and reflect on the conversations ahead—yes, the ones where you actually talk about what you want instead of just texting vague "let's talk about this later" messages. Embrace the chance to sit down with your loved ones and share your hopes, dreams, and maybe even your random quirks (like how you're convinced your collection of rubber bands will be worth something one day). This is an opportunity to strengthen the family bonds and maybe get a few laughs in, too. With some thoughtful communication, you'll ensure your legacy is one of harmony, understanding, and the occasional inside joke—an enduring testament to the love and care that made your life so memorable. Plus, it's way easier than trying to explain why you don't want your cousin's entire collection of porcelain cats passed down as a family heirloom!

Chapter 2

Personal Information Essentials

Who Are You? Documenting Personal Identification

Let's start with the basics. Your full legal name, date and place of birth, and Social Security number are foundational elements of your identity. These pieces of information are not just bureaucratic necessities; they are the building blocks of your personal story. They appear on everything from your birth certificate to your driver's license, and they play a crucial role in legal and financial matters. It's essential to record them accurately, as even a small error—a misspelled name, an incorrect birth date—can lead to a cascade of complications, from delayed legal processes to misplaced assets. Accuracy is paramount, as these details will be referenced by everyone from family members to legal professionals when handling your affairs.

To ensure consistency and precision, I recommend using standardized identification forms. These templates guide you in documenting each piece of information methodically, reducing the risk of oversight. You can use websites such as jotform.com and goformz.com to create your forms or use the ones in my workbook. Most states or local government agencies have an identification form on their websites as well. Think of the forms as checklists that ensure no detail is forgotten. They provide spaces for all necessary data, including middle names and maiden names, which often hold significant importance in legal documents. By using a structured format, you create a comprehensive record that can be easily accessed and understood by those who need it. This approach simplifies the documentation process and provides peace of mind, knowing your information is organized and complete.

Once you've gathered and documented your personal identification details, the next step is to consider secure storage. This information is highly sensitive, and you must protect it from theft or misuse. Fireproof safes provide an excellent option for physical documents as they offer protection against fire and unauthorized access. For those who prefer a digital approach, secure digital storage options are available. Encrypting your data adds an additional layer of security, ensuring that even if accessed, it cannot be easily read or misused. Consider using password-protected files or encrypted USB drives to store digital copies of your documents. These methods safeguard your information, keeping it out of the wrong hands while ensuring it's accessible to those who need it.

Securing your personal data is more relevant today than ever. In a world where identity theft and data breaches are common, taking proactive steps to protect your information is essential. By encrypting your files and using secure storage solutions, you minimize the risk of your data being compromised. Regularly reviewing and updating your security measures further enhances your protection. It's a small investment of time and effort that pays dividends in peace of mind, knowing that your personal information is safe and secure.

> **Call to Action: Personal Data Security Checklist**
>
> Take a moment to review the security measures you have in place for your personal information. Use the checklist below to identify areas where you might enhance your data protection:
>
> - Ensure all sensitive documents are stored in a fireproof safe or encrypted digital format.
>
> - Regularly update passwords and use complex combinations to increase security.
>
> - Consider using password management tools to store and organize passwords securely.
>
> - Encrypt sensitive files and documents to prevent unauthorized access.
>
> - Regularly review and update your security measures to adapt to new threats.

By documenting your personal identification details and securing them effectively, you're protecting your legacy and paving the way for a smoother transition for your loved ones. These steps transform the mundane task of documentation into a meaningful act of care, one that ensures your story continues unencumbered by avoidable complications.

Beyond the Basics: Including Your Unique Identifiers

In personal identification, some details go beyond basic information and become essential when accessing services, traveling, or managing legal matters. Your driver's license number, for instance, is often used as a secondary form of ID, verifying your identity across various platforms. Whether you're opening a new bank account or simply confirming your identity over the phone, this number becomes invaluable. Similarly, your passport details open the world to you, quite literally. Beyond facilitating international travel, your passport serves as a robust proof of identity that's recognized globally. It's a document that not only tells where you've been but also underscores your citizenship and legal standing. For those who have served in the military, a service ID is another layer of identity, unlocking access to veteran benefits, services, and discounts. Each of these identifiers plays a distinct role, ensuring seamless navigation through both routine and extraordinary circumstances.

Incorporating these unique identifiers into your records prepares for any situation where they might be required. Imagine needing to verify your identity quickly during an emergency or while dealing with a government agency. Having these details readily available can save time and reduce stress. It's about anticipating the small moments where having everything in order can make a significant difference. And let's not forget about those specific identifiers that might apply to certain professions or statuses. Professional licenses, for example, are necessary for verifying your qualifications and maintaining your standing in various fields. Whether you're a doctor, lawyer, or even a licensed electrician, these licenses certify your skills and uphold your credibility. Then there are membership IDs for exclusive organizations, which could be anything from a country club to a professional association. These memberships often come with privileges and responsibilities that require proof of identity and status.

When you think about it, these identifiers are more than just numbers or codes; they are the keys to your personal and professional life. They tell a story about who you are, where you've been, and what you've accomplished. They open doors, both literally and metaphorically, and having them well-documented and secure ensures you hold the keys firmly in your grasp. As you compile this information, take a moment to appreciate the breadth of your identity—from your driver's license, which represents your daily independence, to your passport, which signifies your place in the global community. Each piece, when combined, creates a comprehensive picture of you, ready to support and protect you in every facet of life.

Mapping Family Connections: Creating a Family Tree

Creating a family tree is an exploration of your roots, offering insights into who you are and where you come from. A family tree serves as a visual representation of your genealogy, connecting generations and providing a clear picture of your lineage. It helps you understand family dynamics and plays a part in inheritance planning. Knowing who is related to whom can clarify potential legal obligations and inheritance rights, helping avoid disputes that arise from unclear family ties.

To begin constructing your family tree, start with the immediate family. Begin by listing yourself and your closest relatives—parents, siblings, children—those who form the core of your family unit. Include their birthdates, significant life events, and any other relevant details. From there, extend outward to encompass your ancestors, such as grandparents and great-grandparents. Documenting their histories enriches your understanding of familial connections. As you trace back through generations, fill in the gaps with information about marriages, births, and deaths. These connections reveal patterns and relationships that may have been lost over time. As you move forward, add descendants, ensuring you capture the full scope of your family's growth. This is where the tree truly comes to life, illustrating not only where you've come from but also where your family is headed.

The significance of historical context cannot be understated. Family medical histories, for instance, provide vital information that can impact health planning for you and your descendants. Knowing whether certain conditions run in the family allows for better preparedness and preventive measures. Inheritance patterns also become clearer when laid out visually, revealing who traditionally received what and why. This understanding is helpful for estate planning, as it sets expectations and informs decisions on asset distribution. Furthermore, historical context offers a sense of belonging and identity, anchoring you in a lineage that extends beyond your immediate experience. It's a reminder that you are part of a larger narrative, one that has shaped who you are today.

In today's digital world, creating a family tree has never been easier. Genealogy websites and family tree apps offer user-friendly platforms that simplify the process. Websites like Ancestry.com and MyHeritage provide access to extensive databases, helping you track down elusive ancestors and uncover long-forgotten family stories. These platforms often include tools that allow you to upload photos and documents, enriching your tree with visual and textual history. Family tree apps, such as Family Tree Builder or RootsMagic, offer convenience and portability, enabling you to work on your tree from anywhere. These digital tools make it easier to compile and organize information and to share it with family members, encouraging collaboration and collective memory-building.

Emergency Contacts: Who to Call When You're Not There

Think of emergency contacts as your stand-ins when you're not available to make decisions yourself. They are the people who will step in during times of crisis, acting as the bridge between you and the outside world. Designating a primary contact for emergencies is like appointing your personal representative—someone who can provide vital information, communicate with medical or legal authorities, and make decisions in line with your wishes. This person should be someone who knows you well, understands your needs, and can act swiftly and decisively. A secondary backup contact is equally important, serving as an alternate when the primary contact is unavailable. This redundancy ensures that there's always someone ready to take charge, no matter the situation. Choosing the right individuals for these roles requires careful consideration. Reliability is key—your emergency contact should be someone you can count on to be there when needed. Trustworthiness is equally important, as this person will have access to sensitive information and may need to make significant decisions on your behalf. You should look for someone level-headed, able to remain calm under pressure, and willing to take on the responsibility. It's also wise to consider proximity; someone who lives nearby might respond more quickly in an emergency. By selecting individuals who embody these qualities, you ensure that your interests are well-represented and your affairs are managed appropriately.

Documenting these contacts is a straightforward yet important step. Having a structured format for recording their information helps keep everything organized and accessible. Include the contact's name and relationship to you, as this provides context for their role. Capture their phone numbers and email addresses, ensuring they can be reached quickly and through multiple channels. Adding their address for correspondence can also be helpful, especially if legal or medical documents need to be sent. This comprehensive documentation serves as a quick reference in times of need, eliminating confusion and facilitating prompt communication. Regularly updating your contact list is equally important. People's circumstances change, and someone who was once a perfect choice might no longer be available or willing to serve in this role. Conduct annual reviews of your contact list to ensure that all information is current and accurate. During these reviews, reach out to your contacts to confirm their continued willingness to act on your behalf. Involving them in updates reaffirms their commitment and keeps them informed of any changes in your preferences or circumstances. Maintaining this open line of communication ensures that they are prepared to step in confidently when needed.

To ensure your emergency contact information is easily accessible, another step you can take is to set it up in your phone's emergency settings. On most smartphones, you can go to your Health or Emergency section (often in your settings or health app), and add your emergency contacts. Once added, this information can be accessed from your lock screen by first responders or anyone assisting you in an emergency, even if your phone is locked. This quick setup can make all the difference in critical moments.

By carefully selecting and documenting your emergency contacts, you create a support network that stands ready to act when you cannot. This network provides peace of mind, knowing that trusted individuals are equipped to handle emergencies with care and efficiency. As you move forward, consider the broader implications of these preparations. They aren't just about managing emergencies; they are part of a larger effort to ensure that your wishes are respected and your loved ones are taken care of. As we wrap up this chapter on personal information essentials, let's acknowledge that these details form the foundation of a well-organized and thoughtful plan. With your personal and emergency information in place, we can now turn our attention to the next chapter, where we'll explore financial affairs and how to manage them effectively.

Chapter 3

FINANCIAL AFFAIRS SIMPLIFIED

Your finances can easily become like a closet stuffed with clothes from every decade, mismatched shoes, and a random tennis racket that no one in the house has ever used. Now, think about someone else trying to make sense of that mess without you around to explain why there's a stack of unopened bank statements behind the winter coats. Getting your financial affairs in order will spare your loved ones the headache of sorting through chaos when they're already coping with your absence. Let's be honest—nothing says, "I care" quite like a well-organized spreadsheet.

Financial organization doesn't come naturally to most. According to debt.com, only 30% of Americans have a financial plan in place. Yet, having one leads to better money decisions, stability, and peace of mind. We're here to make this less of a chore and more of an accomplishment that brings clarity and control over your financial life.

Banking on Simplicity: Listing Your Accounts

Let's start with your checking and savings accounts. These are the backbone of your financial structure, handling everyday transactions and serving as a reservoir for your savings. Begin by noting the bank name and branch, which helps locate or contact the bank if needed. List the account numbers precisely—these numbers unlock access to your funds. Don't forget the contact information for your account manager, your go-to person for resolving issues or answering questions. This small detail can save a significant amount of time and hassle in the future. Next, consider any joint accounts you might share with family members or partners. These accounts require particular attention because they involve shared responsibilities and access. Document the names of all account holders and any specific conditions or terms associated with the account. Certificates of deposit (CDs) are another aspect. While they might sit quietly accruing interest, you must document them and know when they mature and funds become available again.

Executors and beneficiaries need a clear picture of your financial landscape to manage your estate efficiently. With transparency, they could avoid unnecessary delays or complications, leading to frustration and potential disputes. Your documentation serves as a guide. By providing a clear, detailed account of your financial holdings, you remove guesswork and ensure your wishes will be respected and executed smoothly.

To facilitate this process, consider using structured templates for listing your accounts. Account information sheets provide a consistent format, ensuring that all necessary details are captured for each account. These sheets can be customized to include additional information relevant to your situation, such as online banking credentials or notes about automatic transactions. A sample bank account log can serve as a starting point, offering a template you can adapt to suit your needs. Using these, you create a comprehensive record that is easy to update and share with trusted individuals. Such organization supports financial clarity and empowers you and your loved ones to handle your affairs confidently.

> ### Call to Action: Banking Information Checklist
> Take a moment to create your list of accounts. Use the checklist below to ensure you've covered all bases:
> - Identify all checking and savings accounts, including joint accounts.
>
> - Document the bank name, branch, and account numbers for each account.
>
> - Record contact information for each account manager.
>
> - Include details of any certificates of deposit (CDs), including maturity dates.
>
> - Ensure all information is stored securely – physically and digitally.

You build a solid foundation for your financial planning by listing your accounts and making them transparent. Although seemingly mundane, this task is a cornerstone of responsible economic management. As you complete this section, take a moment to appreciate the peace of mind that comes from knowing your financial affairs are in order.

Investments and Portfolios: Making Sense of Your Assets

When it comes to investments, understanding what you have and how it works is vital. Let's start by sorting your investments into categories, which helps simplify the process and gives you a clear picture of your financial landscape. Begin with stock portfolios, which are collections of stocks you've invested in, hoping they'll increase in value over time. Next, there are mutual funds, which pool money from many investors to purchase a diversified collection of stocks, bonds, or other securities. Professionals manage them, and it can be a less risky investment method. Finally, look at your retirement accounts, such as IRAs and 401(k) plans, designed to help you save for the future. These accounts often come with tax advantages, making them an important part of your long-term strategy. By categorizing these investments, you can better track their performance and make informed decisions.

Once your investments have been categorized, understanding their value is the next step. Current market value is a key term here—it refers to the price at which your assets could be sold in the current market. This value fluctuates based on a variety of factors, including market conditions and economic events. To get a sense of how your investments are performing over time, look at annual performance reports. These reports provide a snapshot of your investments over the past year, showing gains, losses, and overall trends. They help you assess whether your investments meet your financial goals or if adjustments are needed. Keeping track of these values informs your overall financial strategy and helps you understand your portfolio's health.

Risk and diversification are concepts that go hand-in-hand in the world of investing. Risk assessment profiles help you understand the levels of risk associated with different investments. Every investment carries some risk, but the amount varies. Stocks offer high returns but come with greater risk than bonds, which are typically more stable. Diversification is your friend here. By spreading your investments across a range of assets—stocks, bonds, and funds—you reduce the risk of a significant loss. Think of diversification as not putting all your eggs in one basket. It's a strategy that helps protect your investments from market volatility. Understanding these concepts empowers you to build a portfolio that aligns with your risk tolerance and financial goals.

To manage your investments effectively, you can leverage tools and professionals. Financial advisors offer personalized advice tailored to your financial situation and goals. They can help you with complex investment decisions and create a plan that works for you. Additionally, online investment platforms provide convenient access to various investment options and tools. Platforms like Fidelity Investments, highlighted for its expansive product offerings, and Charles Schwab, known for its educational content, offer resources that cater to beginners and experienced investors. These platforms allow you to manage your investments on your terms, with tools for tracking performance, analyzing data, and making trades. They are beneficial for those who prefer a hands-on approach to investing. Whether you choose to work with an advisor or go it alone with the help of technology, the key is to stay informed and actively engaged with your investments.

Insurance Policies: Securing the Future

Did you ever notice that some of the funniest advertisements out there are for insurance? There is a reason for that. Insurance is boring but essential! Insurance policies are like the unsung heroes of estate planning, quietly standing guard to ensure your loved ones are protected no matter what life throws their way. To start, gather all the insurance policies you hold. This includes life insurance, which provides a financial cushion for your family when you're no longer around; health insurance, which covers medical expenses; and home and auto insurance, which protects your most tangible assets. These policies are the safety nets that catch us when we stumble, offering peace of mind that our families won't be left in a financial lurch.

It's essential to document each policy meticulously. Begin with the policy numbers—these are the keys to unlocking benefits when the time comes. Coverage details are equally important, as they outline what's protected and what's not. Understanding these nuances can prevent unwelcome surprises later. Lastly, note down the beneficiary information. These individuals will receive the benefits, and keeping this information current ensures that your wishes are honored without a hitch.

Insurance comes into play in estate planning by providing your loved ones with financial security during a challenging time. Consider life insurance, for instance. It offers a payout that can cover funeral costs, pay off debts, or even provide an income stream to help your family maintain their lifestyle. You need to understand the payout timelines as they inform beneficiaries when they can expect to receive funds. The cost of premiums is another factor to consider. They represent the ongoing investment you make to safeguard your family's future. By staying informed about these details, you ensure that your insurance works for you when it matters most.

Regular policy reviews are a smart way to maintain the adequacy of your coverage. Life changes, such as marriage, divorce, or the birth of a child, can alter your insurance needs. An annual insurance review is an opportunity to assess whether your current policies still align with your circumstances. During these reviews, you may need to adjust your coverage to reflect any changes. Perhaps you've paid off your mortgage and no longer need as much coverage, or you've acquired valuable assets requiring additional protection. By staying proactive in evaluating your policies, you'll ensure they continue to serve your best interests and those of your beneficiaries.

When reviewing your insurance, create a comprehensive policy list. For each policy, include the insurer's name, contact information, and relevant terms and conditions. This list becomes a valuable resource for your executor, simplifying their task and ensuring they have all the information needed to manage your estate effectively. Additionally, consider discussing your policies with your beneficiaries. Open communication helps them understand what to expect and how to proceed when the time comes. These discussions also provide an opportunity to address any questions or concerns, reinforcing the importance of these policies in your overall estate plan.

Comprehensive Insurance Checklist

Personal Insurance

- **Health Insurance**
    - Individual/Family Plans

- Medicare/Medicaid
- Dental Insurance
- Vision Insurance
- Critical Illness Insurance
- Disability Insurance
- Long-Term Care Insurance

- **Life Insurance**
  - Term Life Insurance
  - Whole Life Insurance
  - Universal Life Insurance
  - Variable Life Insurance
  - Final Expense Insurance

- **Auto Insurance**
  - Liability Coverage
  - Collision Coverage
  - Comprehensive Coverage
  - Uninsured/Underinsured Motorist Coverage
  - Personal Injury Protection (PIP)

- **Homeowners/Renters Insurance**
  - Property Damage Coverage
  - Liability Protection

- Personal Property Coverage
- Additional Living Expenses Coverage

- **Travel Insurance**
  - Trip Cancellation/Interruption
  - Emergency Medical Coverage
  - Lost/Damaged Luggage Coverage

Business Insurance

- General Liability Insurance
- Commercial Property Insurance
- Professional Liability Insurance (Errors & Omissions)
- Workers' Compensation Insurance
- Business Interruption Insurance
- Product Liability Insurance
- Commercial Auto Insurance
- Cyber Liability Insurance
- Directors & Officers (D&O) Insurance
- Key Person Insurance

Specialty Insurance

- Pet Insurance
- Wedding/Event Insurance

- Identity Theft Insurance
- Flood Insurance
- Earthquake Insurance
- Umbrella Insurance (Excess Liability)

Investment-Related Insurance

- Annuities
- Guaranteed Income Plans
- Mortgage Protection Insurance

Other Niche Insurance

- Boat/Watercraft Insurance
- Motorcycle Insurance
- RV Insurance
- Farm Insurance
- Aviation Insurance

This checklist is to help you know the many types of coverage available to safeguard yourself, your loved ones, and your assets. Incorporating insurance into your estate will provide your family with a financial buffer against life's uncertainties. It will ensure they'll have the means to deal with the challenges that will arise in your absence, allowing them to focus on healing rather than financial strain. As you reflect on your insurance policies, remember that they are more than just contracts—they are commitments to your loved ones, promises that you will continue to protect them even when you are not there.

Debt and Obligations: Acknowledging Financial Responsibilities

Let's talk about something most of us have in common but rarely enjoy discussing: debt. It's that shadow lurking in the background of our financial landscape, and it has a knack for complicating things if we don't keep it in check. Face it head-on by taking a comprehensive inventory of all your debts. Mortgages and home equity loans often make up most of our debts. They're tied to our most significant asset—our home—so they deserve attention. Next, list your credit card debts. These can pile up quickly with high interest rates, turning manageable balances into daunting figures. Student loans are another common obligation, a reminder of the investment in our education that still requires a payoff. By identifying each debt, you'll create a clear picture of what you owe and to whom.

Once you've listed your debts, managing and reducing them becomes the next challenge. This is where repayment strategies come into play. Consider debt consolidation options if juggling multiple payments feels overwhelming. Consolidation combines your debts into a single payment, often with lower interest rates, making it easier to manage. Alternatively, creating a repayment plan tailored to your financial situation can be effective. Start by tackling debts with the highest interest rates, reducing the overall cost in the long run. Each debt paid off is a step towards financial freedom and a weight lifted from your shoulders. These strategies are not just about eliminating debt; they're about taking control of your financial future.

Debt's impact on estate planning is significant. Outstanding debts need to be settled before any inheritance is distributed. This means the assets you leave behind will first be used to pay off your debts. Debts exceeding assets can lead to insolvency, leaving little or nothing for your heirs. Understanding this dynamic is necessary for planning effectively. Settling debts after death can delay estate settlement, adding stress during a difficult time. By addressing your debts proactively, you minimize the potential impact on your estate and provide clarity for those left to manage your affairs.

For those feeling overwhelmed by debt, resources are available to help. Debt counseling services offer guidance and support, helping you create a plan to manage and reduce your obligations. These services can provide personalized advice tailored to your unique financial situation. Financial planning apps can also be valuable tools in tracking and managing your debt. Apps like RocketMoney, Mint, or YNAB (You Need a Budget) help categorize expenses, set financial goals, and monitor progress, making it easier to stay on track. These resources empower you to take charge of your debt, transforming it from an intimidating figure into something manageable and, eventually, conquerable.

Recognizing and addressing debt is not just an exercise in financial responsibility; it's a vital step in ensuring your legacy is one of stability and forethought. As you deal with your financial obligations, remember that each decision you make today shapes the future for yourself and your loved ones. By approaching debt with a clear plan and utilizing available resources, you're laying the groundwork for a more secure and prosperous tomorrow.

Putting It All Together: Creating a Financial Snapshot

Think of your finances as a detailed summary of your bank account. Each element represents a part of your financial life: assets, liabilities, income, and expenses. When you put them all together, you get a comprehensive overview—your financial summary sheet. Start with your assets, which include cash, property, investments, or even valuable collections. Next, list your liabilities, such as mortgages or credit card debts.

The final step is calculating your net worth. This shows you where your finances stand—whether you're in the positive, or negative, or need to adjust some areas. It's a clear picture of your financial health and can help you understand what's working and what needs attention. So, grab a calculator and dive in—it's an important part of managing your finances.

Creating a financial snapshot is invaluable when decision-making. With a clear picture of your financial status, you can make informed choices about spending, saving, investing, and planning for future goals. It helps you spot trends, track progress, and identify any areas that need improvement. This clarity is especially useful when making major life decisions, such as buying a home, starting a business, or planning for retirement. Understanding your financial situation lets you plan confidently for the future.

However, your financial situation isn't fixed. It changes over time, so it's important to update your financial snapshot regularly. Consider doing quarterly reviews to reassess your finances, update your values, and adjust your plans. These regular check-ins help keep your financial information current, ensuring you can adapt to changes like new income, expenses, or goals. Life events, such as a new job, marriage, or market shifts, may require adjustments to your plans. Keeping your financial snapshot up to date prepares you for whatever changes come your way.

To make compiling and organizing your financial information easier, use structured templates designed for this purpose. These templates ensure consistency and help you capture every detail clearly and understandably. Financial review checklists can also guide you through the process, ensuring you don't overlook any important areas. With a clear and organized financial overview, you lay the groundwork for informed decision-making and proactive planning. This document will guide you toward achieving your financial goals and ensuring your financial affairs are in order. With this foundation in place, you'll be better equipped to deal with the complexities of estate planning, ensuring that your financial legacy is clear and foresightful. As we move forward, this groundwork will be essential in addressing the more intricate aspects of your financial planning and estate management.

Chapter 4

DIGITAL LEGACY MANAGEMENT

You're sitting at your favorite café, savoring your cappuccino like the picture of sophistication, when you can't help but overhear the most bizarre conversation. One person, sounding utterly bewildered, exclaims, "I just found out my dad had 43 online accounts!" The other jumps in with, "That's nothing—my uncle was subscribed to everything from medieval sword forums to gourmet cheese boxes." You do your best to keep your coffee from spraying everywhere, but let's be honest; this chaos is impossible to ignore.

Funny as it sounds, it highlights a real truth of our digital age: our lives aren't just about paper stacks and keys to the family safe anymore. Nope, they're scattered across an online universe of email logins, streaming subscriptions, and maybe even that one app you forgot to cancel after the free trial. This sprawling digital footprint is convenient, but it's also a giant to-do list for future planning. Because while your uncle's cheese subscription is hilarious, your digital life deserves some serious management.

Your digital footprint is essentially the sum of all your online activities. Every email you send, every social media status you update, and every purchase you make contributes to this footprint. Email accounts are perhaps the most central—acting as gateways to other services, and they're used for everything from personal communication to accessing banking information. Online banking profiles, another component, house sensitive financial data and require stringent protection. Then, subscription services range from streaming platforms to monthly deliveries of artisanal coffees. Each service you subscribe to leaves a digital mark, often accompanied by payment details and personal preferences. According to a *Guardian* article, this extensive network of accounts forms your digital estate, a concept often overlooked in traditional estate planning.

Leaving a digital footprint unmanaged can have significant implications. The risks of identity theft loom large, as hackers can exploit unattended accounts to access personal information. An unchecked digital presence also opens the door to unauthorized account access, where cybercriminals might use your details for fraudulent activities. These risks underscore the importance of managing your digital footprint with the same care and attention you would give to your physical assets. You must safeguard your online legacy and ensure your digital life is as secure and organized as your offline one.

Conducting a comprehensive audit of your digital assets is a valuable strategy for managing your footprint. Start by creating an inventory of your online accounts. List each account name, the associated website, and your username or account ID. This inventory will offer clarity about the extent of your digital presence. As you compile this list, take note of any unused or obsolete accounts. These dormant accounts can be vulnerable to breaches, so identifying and closing them is a prudent step. Regularly updating this inventory keeps it current and ensures you maintain control over your digital estate.

To aid in tracking and managing your digital presence, you may want to leverage digital tools and services. Digital footprint monitoring services provide an overview of your online activities, highlighting areas needing attention. These services can alert you to unusual account activity, offering an extra layer of security. Account aggregation apps are another helpful resource. They consolidate information from multiple accounts into a single interface, simplifying management and providing a clear overview of your digital footprint. These tools empower you to stay informed and proactive, enhancing your ability to manage your digital assets effectively.

> **Call to Action: Digital Footprint Inventory Checklist**
> To get started, use the checklist below to begin inventorying your digital accounts:
> - List all email accounts, noting the associated service provider and login credentials.
> - Identify online banking profiles, including the bank name and account access details.
> - Catalog subscription services, highlighting payment methods and renewal dates.
> - Sort through and close any unused or obsolete accounts.
> - Regularly update this inventory to reflect changes in your digital presence.

By understanding and managing your digital footprint, you take a decisive step toward securing your online legacy and ensuring your digital presence reflects your values and wishes, both now and in the future. As our lives become increasingly intertwined with technology, taking control of our digital assets becomes an essential aspect of comprehensive planning.

Passwords and Profiles: Keeping Digital Access Secure

Passwords are the gatekeepers to your online world. They are the first defense against unauthorized access, protecting everything from your bank accounts to social media profiles. The importance of creating complex passwords cannot be overstated. A strong password typically includes a mix of uppercase and lowercase letters, numbers, and special characters, making it difficult for cybercriminals to crack. Yet many still fall into the trap of using simple, easily guessed passwords like "123456" or "password." Each account deserves a unique password as this minimizes the risk of one breach leading to others. Think of your digital presence as a fortress; each password is a lock, and the quality of that lock determines how well-protected your assets are.

However, remembering dozens of complex passwords can be a daunting task. This is where password management tools come into play. These tools are designed to securely store and organize your passwords, ensuring that you can access them easily while keeping them safe from prying eyes. Password manager apps, such as those recommended by *PCMag*, like NordPass and Bitwarden, offer features such as password generation, encrypted storage, and auto-fill capabilities for websites. They act as a vault for your digital keys, requiring you to remember only one master password. Some even alert you to potential data breaches, prompting you to change compromised passwords immediately. Encrypted password lists provide a more manual approach, where you document your passwords in a secure file protected by encryption. This method requires a bit more effort but offers control over storing your information.

Beyond securing your own access, it's important to consider who will manage your digital accounts when you're no longer around. This is where the concept of a digital executor comes into play. A digital executor is a trusted individual you appoint to handle your digital assets after your death. The right person for this role should be tech-savvy, trustworthy, and clearly understand your wishes. Once selected, provide them with detailed access instructions. These should outline how to access accounts, what actions to take (such as closing or memorializing accounts), and your specific preferences. While it's important to provide guidance, avoid including passwords in your will or instructions, as these documents can become public. Instead, make plans to share this information with your appointed executor securely.

Updating passwords regularly is another aspect of maintaining digital security. Passwords should not be static; they require periodic changes to remain effective. Scheduling regular password updates—every three to six months, for example—can thwart attempts by hackers to gain access over time. Using two-factor authentication (2FA) is an additional layer of security that significantly boosts your defenses. With 2FA, even if someone obtains your password, they'll still need a secondary verification code, often sent to your phone, to access your account. This dual-layer approach adds a strong barrier against unauthorized entry. Implementing these practices ensures that your digital presence remains secure and well-guarded.

Reflect on the importance of these measures in protecting your digital life. They will keep your information private and preserve your peace of mind. In a world where data breaches and identity theft are increasingly common, taking proactive steps to secure your passwords and profiles is akin to locking the doors of your home. It's an act of vigilance that safeguards your assets and your personal legacy. As you consider these strategies, remember that digital security is an ongoing process that evolves with technology and the changing digital landscape.

Social Media Afterlife: Handling Online Presences

In the patchwork quilt of our digital lives, social media accounts are those brightly colored squares that shout, "Look! I went to brunch!" But here's the thing—when we shuffle off this mortal coil, those profiles don't just log off. Nope, they hang around, like that friend who refuses to leave the party. Managing these accounts after we're gone is equal parts practical task and emotional rollercoaster, ensuring our digital legacy is less "awkward loose thread" and more "beautiful tribute."

Platforms like Facebook even offer a memorialization option, turning your profile into a virtual shrine where loved ones can share memories and celebrate your life. Think of it as your greatest hits album but without the annoying birthday reminders popping up. On the other hand, Instagram lets your account bow out gracefully, preserving dignity and privacy—no ghost likes. So, it's worth planning whether you prefer to keep your digital footprint alive or let it fade to black. Because even in the afterlife, your online presence deserves a little finesse.

The impact of social media on one's legacy is profound. In many ways, these platforms serve as modern diaries, chronicling our journeys through life. They capture the highs, lows, milestones, and mundane, offering a window into our worlds. Sharing memories and stories through these platforms allows loved ones to reminisce, providing comfort and connection long after we're gone. But it also means that the persona we curated online continues to influence perceptions, shaping how we're remembered. A well-managed social media presence can be a source of solace and a testament to the life lived and the person you were. It underscores the importance of intentionality in managing these digital remnants, ensuring they align with the legacy you wish to leave behind.

Designating social media heirs is an invaluable step in this process. These trusted individuals will oversee your online presence, ensuring your wishes are honored. Platforms like Facebook allow you to set up legacy contacts who can manage your account after you're gone. This role isn't one to be assigned lightly; it requires someone who understands your values and can act in your best interests. You must provide clear guidelines for account management. These instructions should outline your preferences for account status—whether to memorialize or deactivate—and any specific content you wish to highlight or remove. By setting these parameters, you offer your social media heir a roadmap, simplifying their responsibilities and ensuring your digital presence is handled carefully.

Creating templates for social media wishes further streamline this process. These templates capture your preferences in a structured format. For instance, a social media account instruction template might include sections for login details, preferred account status posthumously, and any specific actions to be taken, like deleting certain posts or preserving particular photos. Templates for farewell messages can provide a personal touch, offering space to craft a final message for your online community. This message expresses gratitude, shares a favorite memory, or offers a goodbye, bringing closure to those who follow your digital journey. By documenting these wishes, you ensure that your voice is heard, even in your absence, and that your digital legacy reflects the authenticity of your life.

As we examine the intricacies of our digital afterlife, it becomes clear that each decision shapes the narrative we leave behind. Once a platform for connection and expression, social media becomes a canvas for legacy, capturing the essence of who we are. By taking proactive steps to manage our online presence, we ensure that this legacy is not left to chance but carefully curated to reflect our values, experiences, and cherished memories.

Digital Vaults: Storing and Sharing Vital Information

In the digital security world, digital vaults have become a cornerstone for those seeking to organize and protect sensitive information. Think of a digital vault as a virtual safe—an encrypted, secure online platform to store your most important documents and credentials. These vaults act like a fortress for your data; advanced security measures are used to keep them safe from unauthorized access. Key features often include bank-level encryption, multi-factor authentication, and secure sharing capabilities. They offer a centralized location where everything from legal documents to digital asset credentials can reside, ensuring you have access whenever needed.

When considering what to store in a digital vault, focus on items that are vital to your estate and personal affairs. Legal documents such as wills, trusts, and powers of attorney should take priority. These documents outline your wishes and are necessary for smooth estate management. Financial account details, including account numbers, bank names, and contact information, also belong in your vault. These records ensure that your financial affairs can be managed efficiently without unnecessary delays. Digital asset credentials, like login information for significant online accounts, should also be stored. These credentials are essential for managing your digital presence and ensuring continuity in your digital legacy. By organizing these elements in a single secure location, you simplify access for yourself and those you trust, reducing the risk of losing sensitive information.

Selecting the right digital vault service is an important decision. First, evaluate the security measures each provider offers. Look for vaults that provide robust encryption, such as 256-bit AES, which is considered an industry standard for data protection. Multi-factor authentication is another feature – it adds an extra layer of security by requiring a second form of verification beyond just a password. The vault should also offer secure sharing options, allowing you to grant access to trusted individuals without compromising security. User-friendly interface options are equally important. A digital vault should be intuitive, making it easy to upload, organize, and retrieve information. Some platforms even offer features like automatic reminders for expiring documents or customizable sharing settings, which can enhance usability and convenience.

You'll need to share access to your digital vault to ensure trusted individuals can manage your affairs when you cannot. Setting up access permissions lets you control who can view or edit specific documents within your vault. This feature is handy for delegating tasks or responsibilities to different people, ensuring that each person only has access to the information they need. Designating emergency contacts within the vault is another smart move. These individuals can gain access in urgent situations, ensuring that your affairs are managed smoothly even in your absence. Providing them with clear instructions on accessing the vault and any specific actions they should take helps prevent confusion and ensures your wishes are followed precisely.

Incorporating a digital vault into your planning is like hiring a personal assistant for your legacy—minus the coffee runs and eye rolls. It will keep your vital info safe, sound, and easy to access for the people needing it someday (without them having to play Sherlock Holmes with your email inbox).

With the foundation of digital management carefully laid, we now turn to the tangible aspects of planning. In the next chapter, we will explore the intricacies of healthcare wishes and legal preparations, looking at the documents and decisions that ensure your healthcare preferences are respected and your legal affairs are in order.

You Can Make a Difference

I hope this book is providing clarity, comfort, and actionable steps to help you plan for the future, ensuring peace of mind for yourself and your loved ones. If you are finding value in its pages, I would greatly appreciate it if you could take a few moments to leave a review.

Your feedback not only helps others discover this book but also allows me to continue creating resources that empower and guide people through life's important transitions. Whether it's a brief comment on what is resonating most with you or a detailed reflection on how the book is impacting your planning, your words will make a difference.

To share your review please scan the QR code or visit the link below.

https://www.amazon.com/review/review-your-purchases/?asin=B0DTV456KS

Thank you for taking the time to explore **The Ultimate End of Life Planner** *and for allowing me to be a part of your journey in planning and organizing the important aspects of life.* Your support and encouragement mean the world to me.

With gratitude,
Nicole Reap

Chapter 5

HEALTHCARE WISHES AND LEGAL PREPARATIONS

Health directives instruct your family and doctors when you're unable to speak up for yourself. These legal documents lay out your preferences for medical treatment in case you're ever in a situation where let's say, you're too busy being unconscious to make decisions. Without clear instructions, your loved ones might end up in a panic, trying to guess whether you want to be kept alive on life support or if you'd prefer they just pull the plug and go watch Netflix. Health directives remove the guesswork, giving them guidance in those high-stress moments when emotions are running wild, and your family's trying to remember if you've ever mentioned how you feel about "extreme" measures. In short, they provide a clear, calm roadmap for medical decisions—so no one ends up trying to make a choice that ends with, "Well, I guess we'll just do what we think you would've wanted...?"

Creating a health directive begins with identifying your key medical preferences. Reflect on the types of treatments you are willing to undergo and those you wish to avoid. Consider scenarios such as life-sustaining interventions, resuscitation efforts, and organ donation. Once you've clarified your preferences, the next step is to ensure your directives are legally binding. This typically involves drafting the document in accordance with state laws, obtaining signatures from witnesses, and possibly having the document notarized. By adhering to these legal requirements, you ensure that your directives carry weight and are respected by medical professionals.

Communicating your health directives to family and medical staff is like handing out a detailed instruction manual for when things go south—except no one wants to read it while you're on a gurney. Your family needs to know exactly what you want, so they can be your advocates in the event of a medical emergency. Start by sitting down for some honest talks with your loved ones—this isn't the time for vague "I just want to be comfortable" answers. Be clear about your preferences and why they matter to you. These conversations will help your family understand your wishes, and give them the confidence to step up and say, "Yes, we will honor this, even if we have to fight the medical staff with a giant foam finger." Don't forget to hand over copies of your health directives to your healthcare providers too, so they know exactly what you want in case things get dramatic. Storing copies in easily accessible spots, like your medical records or a digital vault, makes sure your instructions are there when needed—and not buried under a pile of random paperwork you meant to go through "someday."

To assist in articulating your medical preferences, consider using templates that outline common scenarios and options. Sample health directive forms provide a structured approach, guiding you through the process of documenting your wishes. These templates often include sections for outlining treatment preferences, specifying healthcare proxies, and detailing any religious or philosophical considerations that might influence your choices. Examples of common medical wishes, such as do-not-resuscitate orders or preferences for palliative care, can offer inspiration and clarity as you draft your directives. By using these tools, you'll create a comprehensive document that reflects your values and ensures your medical care aligns with your desires.

> **Call to Action: Health Care Reflection**
>
> Take a moment to reflect on your healthcare preferences. Consider what treatments align with your values and which do not. Use your workbook to jot down thoughts and any questions you might have. This reflection will clarify your wishes and prepare you for discussions with family and healthcare providers, ensuring your directives are comprehensive and well-considered. Through thoughtful preparation and clear communication, you'll ensure your healthcare decisions reflect your true intentions and provide peace of mind for both you and your loved ones.

Power of Attorney: Who Will Speak for You?

Power of Attorney (POA) is a legal document that allows you to appoint someone (called your "agent" or "attorney-in-fact") to make decisions on your behalf if you cannot do so yourself. This can cover a variety of areas, such as financial decisions, medical care, or legal matters. There are different types of POA, like a durable POA, which remains in effect if you're incapacitated, and a limited POA, which grants authority only for specific tasks. A financial POA grants the appointed individual, known as the agent, the authority to handle your property and finances. This means they can manage bank accounts, file taxes, and even sell assets if necessary. On the other hand, a healthcare POA, often referred to as a healthcare proxy, empowers the agent to make medical decisions for you. This can include choices about treatments, surgeries, and even end-of-life care. Whether it's financial or healthcare-related, the role of a POA is to act in your best interest, ensuring that your preferences are upheld.

Choosing the right person to hold your power of attorney is a decision that shouldn't be taken lightly. It requires a blend of trust, competence, and understanding. The person you select should be someone who knows you well and can be relied upon to make decisions that align with your values. They should possess the ability to remain calm under pressure, as these situations often arise during challenging times. When appointing a POA, it's essential to have an open and honest conversation with the potential agent, discussing your expectations and any specific instructions you might have. This dialogue will ensure they are prepared to take on the responsibility and understand what is required of them.

Legal requirements for appointment vary by state, but generally, the process involves drafting the POA document, which must be signed in the presence of witnesses or a notary to be valid. This formalization is crucial as without it, the document may not be recognized as legally binding.

The importance of legal documentation in appointing a power of attorney cannot be overstated. A properly executed POA document is your safeguard, ensuring that the authority granted is legitimate and enforceable. Creating this document involves outlining the specific powers you wish to delegate. It's important to consider the scope of these powers carefully, as they will dictate the actions your agent can take. State-specific laws govern the execution of POAs, so it's vital to ensure the document complies with these regulations. Consulting with a legal professional can be invaluable in this process, providing guidance to ensure all legal bases are covered. Once completed, the document should be stored in a secure location, with copies provided to your agent and any relevant third parties, such as financial institutions or healthcare providers.

Despite meticulous planning, challenges can arise once a POA is in place. Disputes may occur if family members disagree with the agent's decisions or question their motives. Open communication is key to resolving such conflicts. Encourage dialogue between the agent and family members to generate understanding and cooperation. If necessary, mediation can be a helpful tool, providing a neutral ground for discussing concerns. Sometimes, circumstances change, and you may need to revoke or alter the POA. This could be due to a change in your relationship with the agent or a shift in your circumstances. The process for revoking a POA typically involves drafting a formal revocation document and notifying all relevant parties. Updating the POA to reflect new preferences or appointing a different agent follows a similar procedure, ensuring that your current wishes are accurately represented.

Living Wills: Your Voice When You Can't Speak

Sometimes situations arise where critical medical decisions need to be made, but you're unable to communicate your wishes. This is where a living will steps in. A living will is a written document that outlines your preferences for medical treatment when you're incapacitated. Unlike a regular will, which deals with the distribution of your assets after death, a living will focuses on your healthcare choices while you're still alive. It guides medical professionals and loved ones, enabling them to honor your wishes, whether it's about life support, resuscitation, or other interventions. Essentially, it's your voice during those times when speaking isn't an option.

Drafting a living will requires careful thought and clarity. Start by specifying your treatment preferences. Consider what types of medical interventions align with your values and which ones you'd prefer to avoid. Common considerations include mechanical ventilation, resuscitation efforts, and artificial nutrition or hydration. Think about your stance on palliative care and pain management. Once you've identified these preferences, document them clearly to avoid any ambiguity. This clarity will ensure that your healthcare providers and family members can interpret your wishes accurately. Including end-of-life care decisions in your living will is equally important. Specify whether you wish to receive life-sustaining treatments in certain situations or if you prefer a different approach, such as comfort care. These decisions reflect your values and beliefs, providing guidance during emotionally charged moments.

Legal considerations ensure your living will is respected. To make it legally binding, the document must comply with your country and your state's laws, which may include specific requirements for signatures and witnesses. It's advisable to review your living will with a legal professional who can ensure it meets all necessary legal standards. This step will safeguard the document's legitimacy and ensure it holds weight in medical settings. Additionally, laws and medical practices evolve, so reviewing your living will periodically is wise. This review ensures your document reflects any changes in your preferences or advances in medical technology. It's an opportunity to reaffirm your choices and make adjustments as needed, keeping your living will a true reflection of your current wishes.

Examples and templates can be invaluable tools when drafting a living will. Sample templates offer a structured framework, guiding you in articulating your wishes effectively. They often include sections for various medical scenarios, providing prompts that help you consider all possibilities. Common clauses might cover preferences regarding resuscitation, organ donation, and the use of experimental treatments. By using these templates, you'll ensure that your living will is thorough and addresses all the important areas. They provide a starting point, allowing you to customize the document to fit your specific needs and values. Reviewing examples of others' living wills can also offer insight and inspiration. They highlight how different individuals approach similar decisions, offering perspective as you craft your own.

> **Call to Action: Living Will**
> Consider reviewing a sample living will template from trusted sources to understand how to structure your document. This template can serve as a guideline, helping you articulate your wishes clearly and confidently. By examining different templates, you'll gain a better understanding of how to express your preferences, ensuring your voice is heard even when you cannot speak.

Living wills are not just legal documents; they are expressions of your deepest values and beliefs. They ensure that your healthcare decisions are respected and provide comfort to your loved ones, knowing they are acting in accordance with your wishes. As you create your living will, remember that it is a "living" document, one that can evolve as your perspectives and circumstances change.

Understanding Advance Directives: Making Informed Choices

Navigating the intricate web of healthcare decisions can be daunting, especially when unforeseen circumstances render you unable to express your preferences. This is where advance directives become invaluable. An advance directive is a legal document that outlines your wishes regarding medical care if you're incapacitated. These directives encompass several components, including living wills and healthcare proxies, each serving a unique purpose. While a living will specifies the types of medical treatments you want or don't want, a healthcare proxy designates someone to make healthcare decisions on your behalf. Understanding the differences and how they work together ensures your medical preferences are respected and followed.

Advance directives ensure your healthcare choices are honored, providing clarity during times of uncertainty. They relieve loved ones from the burden of making difficult decisions without guidance and ensure that healthcare providers have a clear understanding of your wishes. By planning, you take control of your medical care, even when you can't communicate. This foresight aligns treatment with your values and reduces the emotional stress on family members during critical moments. It puts a plan in place that speaks for you, offering peace of mind to both you and your loved ones.

Creating an advance directive is a thoughtful process. Begin by identifying key medical scenarios that concern you. Think about situations like terminal illness, persistent vegetative states, or severe brain injury. Each scenario may require different preferences, so consider your values and beliefs when deciding on the treatments you would want. Next, include specific instructions for these scenarios. Be as detailed as possible, covering aspects like life support, resuscitation, and pain management. These instructions should reflect your convictions and serve as a guide for those tasked with making decisions on your behalf. Once your preferences are clear, formalize your advance directive by following state-specific requirements for signatures and witnesses. This step ensures your document is legally binding and respected by healthcare professionals.

To further your understanding of advance directives, you might wish to explore additional resources. There are numerous books and websites that delve into the nuances of these documents, offering valuable insights and guidance. Websites like the American Bar Association's online resources offer practical tools and templates. These materials not only enhance your knowledge but also empower you to make informed decisions about your healthcare preferences. By equipping yourself with information, you ensure that your advance directive is thorough and reflective of your true intentions, providing a solid foundation for your healthcare planning.

Through the thoughtful creation of advance directives, you lay the groundwork for a healthcare plan that aligns with your values and desires. You're taking proactive steps to ensure your voice is heard, no matter the circumstances. By incorporating these directives into your planning, you're creating a guide for your healthcare providers and loved ones, offering clarity and direction in times of need. As you explore the options available and consider the scenarios that matter most to you, remember that this is an opportunity to shape your healthcare journey, ensuring it reflects your deepest values and beliefs.

Here is a curated list of reputable websites and apps offering templates for advance directives, wills, powers of attorney, and related legal documents:

1. AARP- Provides free, state-specific advance directive forms, including living wills and health care proxies.

2. Legal Templates- Offers customizable templates for various legal documents, such as advance directives and medical powers of attorney.

3. eForms- Features a comprehensive library of legal forms, including advance directives and living wills, with state-specific options.

4. Do Your Own Will- Provides free templates for advance directives, wills, and other estate planning documents.

5. LawDepot- Offers customizable templates for living wills and medical powers of attorney, tailored to individual needs.

6. Five Wishes- A unique advance directive that combines a living will with a health care power of attorney, addressing personal, emotional, and spiritual needs.

7. Advancedirectives.com- Provides free advance directive forms for all 50 U.S. states, including living wills and medical powers of attorney.

8. CaringInfo- Offers free advance directive templates and state-by-state instructions to ensure compliance with local laws.

9. Word Templates Online- Features free templates for advance directives, including living wills and durable powers of attorney for health care.

10. eSign- Provides free advance directive forms in PDF and Word formats, suitable for various needs.

When utilizing these resources, ensure that the templates are valid in your jurisdiction and that you understand the legal requirements for execution in your state.

Legal Contacts: Building Your Support Team

Navigating the complexities of legal planning can feel like wandering through a dense forest without a map. This is where a reliable legal team becomes invaluable. These professionals act as your guides, ensuring that your wishes aren't lost in the thickets of legal jargon and regulations. Lawyers and legal advisors each bring expertise in different areas. Estate planning specialists, for instance, focus on the nuances of managing your assets and ensuring they're distributed according to your desires. They have the knowledge to craft wills and trusts that reflect your intentions, safeguarding your legacy. Additionally, these legal contacts stay updated on laws that might affect your plans, offering timely advice and adjustments to keep everything aligned with your goals.

Selecting the right legal contacts isn't just about picking someone with a fancy degree or a business card that could double as a coaster—it's about finding someone you trust with your most personal affairs. Start by checking their experience, because you don't want someone whose idea of "estate planning" is a game of Monopoly. Look for professionals who have the right credentials and a proven track record in estate planning, especially when it comes to navigating the complicated stuff. Sure, their diplomas may be impressive, but can they explain the fine print without sounding like they're speaking in legalese? Once you've narrowed down your list, conduct interviews to see if you mesh. Ask about their experience with situations like yours and how they handle client communication. A great legal advisor doesn't just talk *at* you—they *listen to you*, offer clear explanations, and present solutions that make sense to you.

Legal contacts ensure that your wishes are legally upheld. They review documents like wills, trusts, and powers of attorney, checking for accuracy and compliance with state laws. This review process is vital, as even minor errors can lead to significant complications. By providing legal advice and updates, these professionals keep your plans current, adapting to changes in your circumstances or the legal landscape. Their guidance helps prevent disputes and ensures that your intentions are executed smoothly. Whether it's clarifying complex legal terms or navigating unexpected challenges, your legal team offers a steady hand, steering you through the intricacies of estate planning with confidence and clarity.

Chapter 6

FUNERAL AND BURIAL PLANS

How do we ensure our final wishes are honored and not left to the imagination of our well-meaning, but occasionally forgetful, relatives? Planning your funeral and burial might feel like trying to plan a party you won't even be at, but trust me, it's an act of love. It will save your family from guessing whether you wanted "a simple cremation" or a Viking funeral with flaming arrows (hey, it could happen). By taking care of the details now, you spare them from the awkward family debates that could arise when they're already juggling grief and catering to Aunt Edna's endless casserole requests.

Final Wishes: Funeral and Burial Preferences

At the heart of planning your final farewell is deciding the type of service that best reflects your beliefs and personality. You might prefer a religious service, rich with tradition and spiritual significance, or perhaps a non-religious ceremony that focuses on celebrating your life through personal stories and shared memories. For those who served in the military, a military service offers a structured, honorific send-off, complete with ceremonial elements that recognize your service to the country. Each choice speaks volumes about who you are and how you wish to be remembered, setting the tone for your final goodbye.

Alongside this, the location holds equal importance. Whether it's a serene chapel, a lively community hall, or a picturesque outdoor setting, the venue should resonate with you and comfort those who gather there.

The participants in your ceremony will be the ones who bring your vision to life. Choosing an officiant who understands your values ensures the service feels personal and sincere. This could be a spiritual leader, a celebrant, or even a close friend skilled in public speaking. Consider who you'd like to speak at your service—perhaps family members, friends, or colleagues who can share anecdotes and tributes that paint a rich picture of your life. Musicians can add a layer of emotion through carefully selected pieces, creating a soundtrack that enhances the mood and reflects your tastes. These choices transform the ceremony from a formal event into a heartfelt celebration of your life.

My friend David's mother passed a couple of years ago. Here is David's account of his mother's end-of-life planning.

"My mother loved to be in control of things. She was a big planner... family vacations, activities for the grandkids, anything you could think of. When she found out she had a terminal illness, she went right into planning mode- this time, for her own memorial service. This was her last opportunity to plan a big event, and she made sure that everything was outlined, down to the smallest details.

She met with the parish pastor to discuss the service, music, and readings. She changed her mind about things a hundred times. She even asked each of her grandchildren who she wanted to speak at the service if they would do so... and wrote them notes to guide them in their eulogies! While all this might seem like an odd way to spend the end of your life, it gave her purpose and kept her busy doing what she loved to do most."

Clarity is your ally in this process. Ambiguity in your instructions can lead to confusion and disputes among family members, detracting from the gathering's purpose. Clear, detailed wishes minimize misunderstandings, ensuring everyone knows exactly what you want. This clarity empowers your family to carry out your wishes confidently, providing them with a guide that prevents unnecessary stress or disagreement. It will give your loved ones a guide, allowing them to focus on celebrating your life rather than worrying about logistics.

Templates for documenting your wishes are invaluable aids in this endeavor. A funeral planning worksheet provides a structured format for capturing your preferences, from the type of service to the music you'd like played. These templates can guide you in detailing every aspect of your funeral, ensuring that nothing is overlooked. Similarly, a sample burial instruction form can help you specify your desires for your final resting place, whether it's a traditional burial site or an unconventional choice like a woodland retreat. These documents serve as a blueprint, making it easy for your family to understand and honor your wishes.

Open discussions with your family are the secret sauce in this whole planning process. Holding family meetings to go over your plans is like hosting a mini town hall—everyone gets a chance to ask questions, voice their opinions, and probably make a few awkward jokes about what music should be played at your memorial. It's your chance to share your written plans with key family members, so they're not left scrambling in confusion when the time comes. By getting them involved, you'll ensure your wishes are crystal clear and reinforce that, yes, you really want that weird, yet sentimental, thing done. These conversations turn what could be an uncomfortable topic into a team effort, helping to strengthen family bonds and giving everyone a little peace of mind—especially when Aunt Linda's already volunteered to make the memorial cupcakes.

Call to Action: Ceremony Wishes

Take a moment to jot down your initial thoughts on the type of ceremony you envision. Consider the atmosphere, location, and who you'd like to be involved. Use this reflection as a starting point for a more detailed plan, and share it with your family to initiate meaningful discussions about your final wishes.

Cremation vs. Burial: Weighing Your Options

Choosing between cremation and burial is a deeply personal decision, often rooted in individual beliefs, family traditions, and practical considerations. Let's start by looking at cremation. This process involves reducing the body to ashes through high-temperature burning, taking about two to three hours. It's generally more cost effective than traditional burial, with prices varying depending on the location and services chosen. Cremation might appeal to those who prefer a simpler, potentially less costly alternative. However, the costs can add up if you opt for additional services like a memorial or viewing, or if you choose an elaborate urn.

Traditional burial involves several steps, including embalming, purchasing a casket, and securing a burial plot. These elements contribute to a higher overall cost, often making burial more expensive than cremation. Burial can also entail long-term costs associated with plot maintenance and headstone upkeep.

Environmental considerations are becoming a bigger factor in the great debate between cremation and burial. While cremation might sound like the "quick and easy" option, it's actually quite energy-hungry, producing about a month's worth of electricity for the average person in carbon dioxide. So, in a way, you're leaving a small carbon footprint... literally. But fear not, technology is on the case! Mercury-filtering equipment is now in place to help reduce some of the nastier emissions. On the other hand, traditional burial might seem like a low-energy choice, but it's not without its own environmental quirks. Embalming fluids can seep into the soil (goodbye, organic garden), and let's not forget the methane emissions from decomposing bodies, which—let's be honest—are not the most pleasant addition to the atmosphere. And of course, burial takes up valuable space and requires ongoing maintenance, turning your final resting place into a bit of an environmental project. For those who are more eco-conscious, there's a greener option: green burials. These eco-friendly options skip the embalming and use biodegradable materials, giving Mother Earth a little love while you take a permanent nap. Understanding the environmental impacts of each choice will help you make a decision that's not only in line with your values but also, hopefully, less likely to leave a literal stink behind.

Cultural and religious beliefs profoundly influence preferences for cremation or burial. In many cultures, burial is a long-standing tradition, deeply tied to rituals that honor ancestors and maintain continuity with the past. For instance, in Judaism and Islam, burial is typically preferred, with specific rites that underscore the sacredness of the body. Conversely, Hinduism traditionally favors cremation, viewing it as a way to release the soul from the physical form. Christianity tends to embrace both practices, with regional and denominational variations. These perspectives offer valuable context as you weigh your options, helping ensure that your choice resonates with your spiritual and cultural identity.

To support your decision-making process, consider using tools like pro-con lists. These can help you weigh the practicalities, costs, and implications of each option, providing a clear overview of what each entails. A questionnaire for personal reflection can also be beneficial, prompting you to consider factors like your environmental concerns, cultural traditions, and emotional comfort with each method. Reflecting on these questions can offer clarity, ensuring that your decision aligns with your personal values and priorities. By approaching this choice thoughtfully, you ensure that your final arrangements reflect the life you've lived and the legacy you wish to leave behind.

Personalizing the Ceremony: Reflecting Your Life

Your life is a rich collection of experiences, relationships, and passions that have made you who you are. When it comes to your final send-off, personalizing the ceremony will transform it from a generic event into a meaningful celebration of your unique journey. It's a chance to honor your life as you say goodbye. Think about including those quirky personal stories—the time you bravely scaled a mountain (or at least tried), the community project you started, or how you made the best apple pie the neighborhood ever tasted. These stories, shared by your closest friends and family, will turn your ceremony into a heartfelt reflection of your life. You can make sure your final moment isn't just a ritual, but a true reflection of the person who made memories—and perhaps a few people laugh along the way.

Music and readings set the tone and mood of the ceremony. Choosing pieces that reflect your personality can evoke memories and emotions more powerfully than words alone. Perhaps a favorite song that you danced to during joyous occasions or a poem that you found solace in during challenging times. These selections become a soundtrack to your life, underscoring the moments that defined you. Imagine a ceremony where the opening notes of your wedding song float through the air, or where a passage from your beloved novel sets the scene. These elements won't just fill the silence; they'll speak volumes about who you are, offering comfort and connection to those present.

When it comes to personalizing your ceremony, creativity truly has no limits—because why not go out with a bang (or at least a really memorable theme)? Themed funerals or celebrations of life are a great way to make sure your send-off is as unique as you are. Are you a gardening enthusiast? Picture a ceremony surrounded by blooming flowers, where guests can plant seeds in your memory—just hope they don't forget to water them! For the sports fan, why not have your favorite team's colors in the décor, with memorabilia as centerpieces? That way, even in the afterlife, you're still winning trophies. If travel was your thing, how about a service with postcards and souvenirs from your global adventures? It'll give everyone a tactile connection to your wanderlust—minus the jet lag. Incorporating your hobbies and passions into the ceremony will make it a reflection of you and create a space for your loved ones to laugh, reminisce, and share stories about the things that brought you joy. After all, who wouldn't want to be remembered for their best moments?

Involving family and friends in the planning process is another layer of personalization that will enrich the ceremony. Assigning roles to family members empowers them to contribute meaningfully. A sibling might share a cherished memory, while a close friend could read a passage that encapsulates your spirit. Inviting friends to share memories creates a mosaic of perspectives, painting a fuller picture of your life. This collaboration fosters a sense of community, allowing those present to feel intimately connected to the ceremony's narrative.

To facilitate this personalization, consider using templates designed to help document and organize the unique elements of your ceremony. A personalization planning guide offers a structured approach to capturing your preferences, from the music and readings to the thematic elements that reflect your life. These templates ensure that every detail is considered and communicated, offering clarity to those tasked with bringing your vision to life. A checklist for unique ceremony elements may be helpful, ensuring that nothing is overlooked and that each component aligns with your wishes. By taking the time to personalize your ceremony, you're creating a memorable farewell and crafting a legacy that reflects the richness and diversity of your life.

Writing Your Obituary: It's Your Story to Tell

You can have the final say in how your life is portrayed. An obituary is much more than a mere announcement of a passing; it serves as a testament to the life you led, encapsulating achievements, milestones, and personal stories in a way that resonates with those you leave behind. It's the narrative of your journey, a story that captures both the facts and essence of who you were. By writing your own obituary, you take control of your legacy, ensuring that your values and personality shine through the words that will be shared with the world.

Crafting a personal obituary is your chance to shine one last time and highlight the key events that made your life uniquely yours. Think about the big moments—maybe the day you graduated, moved to a new city, or had that memorable first day as a parent (we all know how that goes). These milestones are the chapters in your story that show how you lived and the decisions that shaped you. But it's not just about the major events;

it's also about injecting some personality into your narrative. Were you known for your wit, your kindness, or your unrelenting need to go on spontaneous adventures (even if it was just a 3-day weekend road trip with questionable snacks)? Let those traits shine through, and don't be afraid to add some color and humor to your story. After all, this is your last chance to leave a mark—and to make sure your obituary isn't just a dry list of facts, but a reflection of the real, funny, and uniquely *you* person you were.

When writing an obituary, certain elements are commonly included to ensure completeness. Begin with the basic announcement of your passing, providing details such as your name, age, and date of death. This sets the stage for the story that follows. Including surviving family members offers a connection to those who remain, acknowledging the bonds that endure. Memorial service details provide information about the ceremony celebrating your life, offering loved ones an opportunity to gather and pay their respects. Consider including charitable donations in lieu of flowers, guiding well-wishers toward causes that were close to your heart. This choice transforms sympathy into action, creating a legacy of giving that will continue in your absence.

To assist in crafting your obituary, you could use sample formats and creative writing prompts. Sample obituaries offer a structured approach, guiding you in organizing your thoughts and ensuring all necessary components are included. These templates provide a framework that simplifies the process, reducing the overwhelm that can accompany writing about oneself. Creative writing prompts can spark inspiration, helping you explore different aspects of your life and articulate them meaningfully. Whether it's listing your top achievements, reflecting on lessons learned, or expressing gratitude to those who supported you, these prompts encourage introspection and creativity.

Writing your own obituary might seem like a task fit for the truly morbid, but it's actually a golden opportunity to shape your legacy—and let's be real, you've earned the right to tell your story your way. It's like a personal highlight reel, minus the awkward editing. Think about it: you get to reflect on the best moments of your life, celebrate your achievements, and ensure your story doesn't get lost in the shuffle of generic obits that read like a shopping list. By taking the time to write your own narrative, you're giving your loved ones a gift—a no-fuss, no-guesswork account of who you were that they can cherish and share. This final narrative will serve as a lasting reminder of your impact, the laughs you shared, and, hopefully, the fact that you were that person who always brought the best snacks to the party.

I have heard many stories of how planning for your death and the details of your funeral can make a huge difference on your loved ones when you pass. Here are two examples of how planning for your passing is the greatest gift you can leave your loved ones. First, here's Sharron's Story:

"Caring for an elderly parent at the end of life is one of the most challenging experiences. My mom was eccentric, fun-loving, and deeply involved in our lives. She led Girl Scouts, supported Toys for Tots, and helped anyone in need. Her generous spirit defined her, and she often urged my sister and me to write a book about our lives, a suggestion we laughed off—but here I am now, writing.

When our dad passed from kidney failure, we faced unexpected challenges due to his lack of end-of-life planning. Despite selling life insurance, he had no policy in place for himself, leaving us scrambling to arrange his funeral. Determined not to leave us in the same position, our mom pre-paid her funeral expenses, secured her burial plot next to our dad, and documented her wishes for her final arrangements. She even planned her funeral as a festive Christmas party, complete with a white elephant gift exchange and Christmas music, reflecting her lifelong love of the holiday.

Years later, she was diagnosed with dementia and Alzheimer's, though she remained active and avoided medications she referred to as "drugs." In the early stages of her illness, she communicated her end-of-life directives, ensuring we knew her wishes regarding life support and medical care. Her thoughtful planning lifted a tremendous emotional and financial burden from us, reinforcing the importance of preparing for the inevitable—for ourselves and our loved ones."

My friend Nancy had a similar experience with her mother. Nancy's mother lived a remarkable life, staying active well into her later years, even after breaking her hip at the age of 104. A thoughtful and practical woman, she understood the importance of estate planning and took deliberate steps to ease the burden on her family after her passing. Knowing that life's final chapter comes for everyone, she carefully planned every detail of her funeral, ensuring her family could focus on celebrating her life rather than managing logistical concerns.

She chose the dress she would wear—a cherished outfit from her grandson's wedding—and even wrote and prepaid for her obituary. A passionate genealogist, she authored a book on a branch of her family's history, leaving behind a lasting legacy. She prearranged her funeral service, budgeting every aspect from the preacher's fee to the flowers, using the same funeral home her parents had. She even selected her casket and specified the flower spray she wanted. Family heirlooms were thoughtfully assigned, with a list detailing who would receive which treasured items.

Nancy described the experience as walking into a Thanksgiving dinner where everything was already prepared. While her mother's passing was still deeply painful, the meticulous planning lifted the heavy administrative burden. Surrounded by love, her mother passed peacefully at Nancy's home, leaving behind not just cherished memories but also a final gift of thoughtful preparation and grace.

As we wrap up this chapter on funeral and burial plans, remember that each step you take in planning is an act of care for yourself and your loved ones. You're ensuring that your wishes are respected and your life celebrated with authenticity. This thoughtful preparation paves the way for a meaningful farewell, one that reflects the person you've been and the legacy you wish to leave. As we move forward, we'll explore the tangible aspects of estate planning, where these thoughtful preparations come together to form a cohesive plan for the future.

Chapter 7

Property and Real Estate

Real estate, whether it's the home you live in, a vacation retreat, or a rental property, represents a significant portion of your wealth and legacy. Documenting these assets comprehensively ensures they are managed effectively and passed on smoothly. This will create a clear picture of your assets that will prevent future disputes and confusion.

Home Sweet Home: Documenting Real Estate

Let's start with cataloging your real estate holdings. Whether you own a cozy bungalow or a sprawling estate, you must document every property you own. Begin with your primary residence. This is your castle, your sanctuary, and likely your most significant asset. Note down the address, purchase date, and original purchase price. These details tell the story of your home but more importantly, provide essential information for tax purposes and potential sale considerations. Next, move on to any vacation homes. These properties might not be your everyday abode, but they hold memories and often represent a substantial financial commitment. Document them with the same thoroughness, ensuring that future generations understand their value and significance.

If you own rental properties, the documentation becomes even more important. Rentals are not just assets; they are income generators, each with its own set of responsibilities and legal obligations. Record the address, tenant details, lease agreements, and current rental income. This comprehensive record helps in managing these properties efficiently and ensures that any transition of ownership is seamless. You need to create a detailed inventory that captures the full scope of your real estate portfolio, providing clarity for you and your heirs.

Now, let's look at the importance of including property details. Each property should have a detailed record that includes addresses, purchase dates, and current mortgage information. You need to know what you owe, the interest rate, and the remaining term on your mortgage. This information is necessary for estate planning, as it affects the net value of your properties and your overall estate. By documenting these details, you provide a clear financial picture that aids in decision-making and ensures that executors and beneficiaries will be able to handle your estate efficiently.

Thorough documentation of real estate holdings isn't just a best practice—it's an absolute must. Without it, you're basically setting up your heirs for a game of *Who Gets the House?* that could rival any reality TV drama. Imagine your siblings squabbling over who gets the family home, all because you didn't bother documenting your wishes. Suddenly, what should have been a simple inheritance turns into a legal battle with all the drama and none of the commercial breaks. By keeping everything documented, you remove the guesswork and give your heirs clear instructions to follow. This clarity will ensure your executors can fulfill your wishes without breaking a sweat—or calling in the lawyers.

To assist in organizing this information, consider using property information sheets. These structured templates will guide you in capturing all the necessary details for each property. They include sections for addresses, purchase prices, mortgage data, and any other relevant information. Sample real estate inventory forms can also be incredibly helpful. These forms act as a checklist, ensuring that no detail is overlooked. They provide a consistent format that makes updating and reviewing your property information straightforward.

> **Call to Action: Real Estate Inventory Checklist**
> To get started on your real estate documentation, use the checklist below to ensure you've covered all the bases:
> - List each property you own, including primary residences, vacation homes, and rental properties.
> - For each property, document the address, purchase date, and original purchase price.
> - Include current mortgage information, such as remaining balance, interest rate, and term.
> - For rental properties, record tenant details, lease agreements, and rental income.
> - Use property information sheets and sample inventory forms to organize and update this information regularly.

Deeds and Titles: Understanding Ownership

Deeds and titles are the backbone of property ownership, yet they are often shrouded in legal jargon that leaves many scratching their heads. Understanding these documents is important because they establish your claim to a property, much like a birth certificate verifies your identity.

A deed is a legal document that transfers property ownership from one party to another. It includes details about the buyer, seller, and property itself, and is often signed in the presence of a notary to ensure legality. Meanwhile, the title represents the legal right to own, use, and sell the property. Think of the title as the concept of ownership, while the deed is the physical proof of that ownership. Together, they form a duo that confirms your stake in your home, vacation retreat, or rental property.

Accessing and reviewing your property documents should be at the top of your to-do list—whether you're buying, selling, or just trying to avoid the chaos of misplaced records. Step one: contact your local land records office, where the magic happens. These offices are like the DMV of the real estate world—except, hopefully, less of a time-suck. They keep all your public records of deeds, titles, and other documents. When you call them up, be ready with info like the property address and parcel number—because they can't just "look it up" like your favorite pizza place. Many offices now offer online databases for deed searches, which is a game-changer. You can verify everything without ever having to put on pants or leave your couch. And the best part? You can print copies of deeds and titles to ensure you're not getting outdated information, making you look like a savvy property owner. Regularly reviewing these documents is like taking your real estate vitamins—it prevents future headaches and catches any pesky errors before they snowball into expensive legal messes. Better safe (and organized) than sorry!

Understanding the different forms of property ownership is another aspect of managing your real estate. Joint tenancy is a common arrangement where two or more people own a property together, each with equal rights and responsibilities. If one owner passes away, their share automatically transfers to the surviving owner(s), bypassing probate. This can be a convenient option for couples or family members. Tenancy in common, on the other hand, allows multiple owners to hold distinct shares of a property. Each share is inheritable, meaning it can be passed on to heirs, making it ideal for co-owners who want flexibility in their estate planning. Community property is a form of ownership recognized in certain states, where all property acquired during a marriage is considered jointly owned, regardless of whose name is on the title. Understanding these distinctions helps you choose the best arrangement for your needs, whether you're buying a property with a partner or planning your estate.

Ownership disputes can pop up even in the friendliest of situations, so it's a good idea to have a few strategies up your sleeve, just in case.

Mediation is a great starting point—it's the "talk it out" method but with a neutral third party acting as the referee. It's usually faster and cheaper than dragging the situation to court, where you'll probably end up paying for a lot of lawyer's coffee instead of actually solving the problem. If mediation doesn't do the trick, then you might need to call in the big guns: a property lawyer. They'll help you navigate the legal labyrinth, giving you the clarity you need without making you feel like you're starring in your own courtroom drama. Another way to avoid all this drama is by keeping your ownership records up to date. Whether you've sold a property, inherited it, or gone through a divorce, making sure those changes are documented pronto helps keep things clear—and keeps your family from fighting over who gets what in the future.

Incorporating these practices into your real estate management protects your interests and lays the groundwork for a more secure and transparent future. Understanding deeds and titles, and how they interact with the various forms of ownership, equips you with the knowledge needed to manage your properties effectively. Accessing and reviewing your documents regularly keeps you informed and prepared for any changes or challenges that may arise. By addressing potential disputes proactively and maintaining up-to-date records, you create a foundation of trust and clarity for yourself and any co-owners or heirs.

Valuing Your Assets: Real Estate Appraisals

Understanding the true value of your property is more than just satisfying curiosity or impressing the neighbors—it's a fundamental aspect of managing your real estate assets. Real estate appraisals provide an accurate picture of a property's market value, which is essential when making informed decisions about your estate. Whether you're considering selling, refinancing, or planning your estate, knowing the current market value can guide you in making choices that align with your financial goals. An appraisal assesses various elements such as the property's size, location, and condition, ultimately providing a valuation that reflects its worth in the current market. This valuation influences inheritance decisions, as it helps determine the equitable distribution of assets among heirs. By understanding the property's value, you ensure that your estate plan is based on accurate and up-to-date information, minimizing disputes and ensuring fairness.

When it comes to obtaining an appraisal, it's important to choose the right professional. Look for a certified appraiser who is familiar with the local market and has a track record of thorough, accurate assessments. A certified appraiser is someone who has met specific educational and professional requirements, ensuring they have the skills needed to evaluate property accurately. You can use resources like the "Find an Appraiser" online directory to locate qualified professionals in your area. Once you've selected an appraiser, it's important to understand the appraisal process. This typically involves an on-site inspection, where the appraiser evaluates the property's condition, measures its dimensions, and takes note of any unique features. The appraiser then compares the property to similar ones in the area that have recently sold, adjusting for differences to determine the market value. This process ensures that the appraisal reflects the property's true worth, considering all relevant factors.

Several factors can influence a property's value, and understanding these can help you anticipate and interpret appraisal results. Location is perhaps the most significant factor, as properties in desirable neighborhoods or with proximity to amenities often command higher prices. The condition of the property also affects the value—well-maintained homes with modern features and updates are typically valued higher than those needing repairs or upgrades. Additionally, market trends and economic factors can impact valuations. During periods of strong economic growth, property values tend to rise, while economic downturns can lead to decreased demand and lower prices. Keeping an eye on these trends can help you make strategic decisions about when to buy, sell, or hold your property.

To effectively document and track your appraisals, you could use appraisal summary sheets. These templates provide a structured format for recording details from each appraisal, such as the appraiser's name, the date of the appraisal, and the final market value. Summary sheets offer a clear and concise overview, making it easy to reference past appraisals when needed. Comparison charts for multiple properties can also be useful, especially if you own several real estate assets. These charts allow you to compare appraisals side by side, highlighting differences in value and helping you identify trends or patterns. By organizing your appraisal information in this way, you create a resource that supports informed decision-making and effective estate management.

> **Call to Action: Appraisal Reflection Section**
> Reflect on your property's value and its role in your overall financial strategy. Use the following prompts to guide your thoughts:
> - How does the current market value of your property align with your long-term financial goals?
> - Are there improvements or upgrades that could enhance the property's value before your next appraisal?
> - How do recent market trends influence your decision to buy, sell, or hold your real estate assets?

Reflecting on these questions helps you align your real estate strategies with your financial objectives, ensuring your property assets support your broader goals.

Sharing and Inheriting Property: Avoiding Family Feuds

Imagine this: a cozy family gathering around the dinner table, nostalgia in the air—until the first sibling declares, "I should get the lake house!" Suddenly, the table turns into a battlefield, with each sibling staking their claim on the beloved property like it's the last piece of pizza. What should be a peaceful moment of remembrance quickly morphs into a full-blown showdown. This is a classic example of the chaos that can unfold during property inheritance. At the heart of these disputes? Unequal asset distribution. One sibling might feel completely cheated if another gets the family home, which they've somehow convinced themselves is worth more than the entire collection of heirloom china. Emotions run high, and before you know it, everyone's arguing over who deserves what, which makes it practically impossible to come to a fair resolution. Many of these conflicts could be avoided with some solid communication and planning, so no one feels left out or like they're playing the role of the villain in a family drama.

It is important to develop strategies for equitable property distribution that ensure fairness and transparency. A property distribution plan involves clearly outlining how assets will be divided among heirs. This plan should consider both the sentimental value and financial worth of properties, ensuring each heir receives a fair share. Open discussions with family members about their preferences and expectations can help align the plan with everyone's needs, reducing the risk of disputes.

Utilizing trusts to manage inheritance is another effective strategy. Trusts allow for a structured approach to asset distribution, with conditions on how and when assets are inherited. This is particularly beneficial when heirs are young or need guidance in managing their inheritance. Establishing a trust creates a flexible framework that protects assets and ensures they are distributed according to your wishes.

When it comes to inheriting property, the legal and financial considerations are more important than you might think—especially if you don't want your inheritance to end up as a family feud in court. First off, understanding estate taxes is essential because these can seriously take a bite out of your heirs' newfound fortune. Estate taxes are like that unexpected surprise at the end of a party—the fun's over when you realize the government wants its cut. Depending on the size of the estate and where you live, these taxes can really take a chunk out of the inheritance your heirs were expecting. You must plan for this. If you're unsure, seek advice from a tax professional.

Take it from my friend Michelle, who inherited her grandmother's house—a beautiful old place with a wraparound porch, but not much else. Michelle was thrilled until she learned about the hefty estate tax that came with it. After some very tense phone calls with the IRS (during which Michelle considered calling in a voodoo priestess), she learned the hard way that if her grandmother had planned ahead, it could have spared Michelle a whole lot of headaches.

Then there's the legal documentation—updating deeds and titles to reflect the new ownership is no small task. You may need to file these documents with local authorities, making sure everything is officially transferred and, most importantly, in writing. Proper documentation ensures a smooth transition and keeps your property out of the "Who's Really in Charge?" saga that can arise when things are left unclear. So, take the time to dot your i's and cross your t's.

Here are a few more real-life examples of how important property planning is for your family. Consider the case of the Johnson family, who faced potential conflict over their grandparents' farm. By working with a mediator and developing a detailed distribution plan, they managed to divide the property amicably, with each sibling receiving a portion that reflected both their needs and the farm's sentimental value.

Another lesson comes from the Martinez siblings, who used a trust to oversee the distribution of their late mother's rental properties. This approach allowed them to manage the properties collectively, providing a steady income stream while preserving the family legacy. These examples illustrate that with careful planning and communication, property inheritance can be handled smoothly, preserving family harmony and honoring the deceased's wishes.

As we wrap up this chapter on property and real estate, let's consider how these discussions fit into the broader context of your planning efforts. By addressing the challenges of property inheritance and implementing strategies for equitable distribution, you're taking important steps to ensure your legacy is passed on with clarity and fairness. This foundation will support your heirs and strengthen family bonds, creating a legacy of unity and understanding. In the next chapter, we'll explore how to craft personal messages and legacies that resonate with your loved ones, ensuring that your values and stories continue to inspire future generations.

Chapter 8

Legacy and Personal Messages

Words to Remember: Crafting Personal Messages

Personal messages hold the unique ability to transcend time, offering comfort and clarity to loved ones after we are gone. Your words can be a guiding light, providing solace during moments of uncertainty or grief. Whether it's a simple "I love you" or a detailed recollection of a cherished memory, these messages can become touchstones for those who might feel adrift without your presence. In a world often consumed by the immediate, the permanence of a written or recorded message offers a rare sense of continuity. By sharing heartfelt sentiments, we extend a part of ourselves, ensuring that our presence is felt even in our absence.

Crafting a message that resonates requires a thoughtful approach. Begin with heartfelt language that will speak directly to the recipient's heart. Imagine sitting across from them, sharing these thoughts in a warm and familiar setting. Choose a tone that feels authentic to your relationship, whether it's light and playful or serious and reflective. The language should reflect the unique bond you share, capturing the essence of your connection. Avoid overly formal language that might create distance; instead, opt for words that are genuine and sincere. Remember, the goal is to provide comfort, understanding, and encouragement. Your message should serve as a balm, soothing the soul and offering a sense of peace.

While written letters are timeless, consider exploring other creative formats to deliver your messages. Video recordings capture your words and your expressions and tone, adding a new dimension to your communication. Your loved ones will probably appreciate hearing your voice, seeing your smile, and feeling your warmth long after you've left this world. Similarly, audio messages can provide a personal touch, allowing your voice to resonate in their ears. If you're artistically inclined, a memory book or scrapbook can serve as a visual journey through shared experiences. These formats offer a tangible connection, transforming your message into a cherished keepsake that can be revisited time and again.

Here are a few examples to inspire your creativity. A message to a child might include words of love and encouragement, reminding them of their potential and the pride you feel in their accomplishments. "Dear Alex, know that you have a kind heart and a brilliant mind. Trust yourself and follow your dreams, for you have everything you need to succeed." For a spouse, a message of gratitude can express appreciation for shared experiences and the bond you've cultivated. "To my beloved, thank you for the love, laughter, and adventures we've shared. You have been my partner in every sense, and my heart is forever grateful." These examples illustrate the power of personal messages to convey deep emotions and lasting love.

> ### Call to Action: Creating Your Message
> Take a moment to reflect on those you wish to leave messages for. Consider the unique qualities of your relationship and the sentiments you wish to convey. Use the prompts below to begin crafting your message:
> - Reflect on a cherished memory or shared experience.
> - Consider the values or advice you want to impart.
> - Think about the emotions you want to evoke in your recipient.

With these reflections in mind, start drafting your message in the format that feels most authentic. Remember, your words are a gift—a lasting testament to the love and connection you share with those who matter most.

Lasting Legacies: Passing on Values and Traditions

The legacy you leave behind isn't just material assets or wealth. They're also the values and beliefs that define who you are. These core values shape your decisions, influence your relationships, and ultimately, create the legacy you leave for future generations. Documenting them can be as simple as jotting down guiding principles or as detailed as writing a manifesto of beliefs. Consider what has been most important to you in life—perhaps it's integrity, kindness, or perseverance. By clearly articulating these values, you offer a roadmap for your loved ones, guiding them through life's challenges with your wisdom as their compass.

Preserving family traditions maintains a sense of continuity and belonging. Traditions, whether they're elaborate holiday celebrations or simple Sunday dinners, provide a rhythm to life that grounds us in familiarity. They are the rituals that bring us together, offering comfort and consistency amidst life's unpredictabilities. One way to ensure these traditions endure is to create a family traditions guide. This can outline the rituals that have been meaningful to your family, detailing how they are celebrated and why they matter. Hosting regular family gatherings or ceremonies can also reinforce these traditions, creating opportunities for shared experiences and memories. These gatherings need not be extravagant; even a casual potluck can become a cherished tradition, strengthening family ties with each shared meal.

Storytelling is a wonderful way to convey values and heritage. Through stories, we pass down lessons learned, experiences lived, and wisdom gained. Writing a family history can capture these narratives, preserving them for future generations. This history doesn't have to be a formal document; it can be a collection of anecdotes, reflections, and even humorous tales that paint a vivid picture of your family's journey. Recording oral histories is another way to keep these stories alive. Sitting down with a loved one and capturing their stories on tape can offer insights into their lives and perspectives, creating a treasure trove of memories that can be passed down. These stories serve as a bridge between generations, connecting the past with the present and ensuring that your legacy continues to inspire and guide.

In this digital age, there are numerous resources available to help document and share your legacy. Legacy journals provide a space to record thoughts, values, and memories, creating a tangible record of your life. These journals can be as structured or as freeform as you like, allowing you to express yourself in a way that feels authentic. Online family history platforms offer another avenue for preserving and sharing legacies. Websites like Ancestry.com and MyHeritage allow you to upload family trees, photos, and documents, creating a digital archive accessible to family members worldwide. These platforms preserve history and facilitate connections, enabling family members to collaborate on building a shared legacy.

Nature's Legacy: Our Family Cookbook

Last year, my sister-in-law gave everyone in our family a cookbook full of family recipes. I asked Nature what had inspired her to create it. Her words capture the story of a legacy so beautifully:

"Many of my fondest memories revolve around the kitchen, where I would watch my father, grandmother, mom, and others cook their favorite dishes for our family. The special times we shared around the table, catching up with one another, are memories I hold dear in my heart and mind. Years ago, my husband and started our estate planning. This difficult process had me reflecting on what would happen after I was gone and what I wanted our children to remember—not just about my husband and me, but also about our family members who had already passed."

"That's when the idea of creating a family cookbook came to me! I reached out via email to close and distant relatives from both my family and my husband's, asking them to share their favorite recipes, especially those passed down from their parents or grandparents. The responses I received were not just recipes, but also heartfelt stories with sentimental backstories attached to them. Creating this cookbook turned out to be incredibly rewarding. Once I'd gathered enough recipes, I decided to organize some of them by holidays. I thought this would help our now-adult children prepare for their own celebrations while reminding them of our past family gatherings and the wonderful times we had together. After a few years of hard work, the cookbook was finally complete, and during the holidays, I gifted the books to our family. It was a priceless gift that touched everyone deeply. I felt an overwhelming sense of peace and contentment, knowing that a precious part of our family history was now preserved for generations to come."

> **Call to Action: Creating Your Family Traditions Guide**
>
> Consider the traditions that have been meaningful to you and your family. Use the prompts below to begin crafting a family traditions guide:
>
> - Reflect on the traditions that have been most significant in your life.
>
> - Consider how these traditions can be adapted or expanded for future generations.
>
> - Think about ways to involve family members in preserving and celebrating these traditions.

Start by documenting these traditions, noting their origins, significance, and any special elements that make them unique. Share this guide with your family, encouraging them to contribute their own memories and ideas. In doing so, you create a living document that evolves with your family, preserving the essence of your legacy for years to come.

Family Heirlooms: Deciding Who Gets Grandma's Vase

Family heirlooms hold a special place in our hearts, acting as tangible links to our past and the stories that shaped us. Imagine opening a dusty old box to find your grandmother's vase, its delicate patterns whispering tales of family gatherings and celebrations long past. Such items often carry symbolic meanings, transcending their material value to embody family history and cherished memories. They serve as reminders of where we come from, encapsulating the lives and experiences of those who walked before us. In many ways, heirlooms are more than just objects; they are storytellers, bridging generations and preserving the essence of family heritage.

When it comes to deciding who should receive a cherished heirloom, the task can feel daunting. The key is to consider the sentimental value of each item and how it aligns with the personalities and interests of potential recipients. You might ask yourself, "Who will appreciate this item the most?" or "Who has a special connection to this piece?" For instance, a family quilt might belong with the relative who spent summers learning to sew with Grandma, while the grandfather clock might find its place with someone who shares the original owner's love for meticulous craftsmanship. Matching heirlooms with personalities ensures that these items continue to be cherished. You'll hopefully avoid disputes over heirlooms and keep the family peace—avoiding the dreaded "Who gets Grandma's rocking chair?" showdown. Getting the family involved in the decision-making process can create a sense of fairness and inclusion (and probably save you from playing referee later). Why not host a family meeting where everyone gets a chance to voice their preferences and explain why they *really* need that vintage lamp or the creepy collection of porcelain dolls? This open conversation can help prevent those "Why didn't you tell me you wanted it?" moments and turn what could be an awkward situation into a shared celebration of family history (or at least a funny story for future gatherings). And don't forget written agreements—because nothing says, "We're serious" like a formal document! By putting everything in writing, you create a crystal-clear record that can keep things from getting messy down the road. That way, when Aunt Sandy starts talking about "her" antique tea set, you'll have the paperwork to back it up and keep the peace.

Consider the story behind a family quilt, passed down through generations. It began as a wedding gift, lovingly stitched by a grandmother for her granddaughter. Over the years, it warmed the beds of children and comforted loved ones during times of loss. Each patch tells a story of its own, from the fabric of a christening gown to a piece of a well-loved dress. The quilt is more than just a blanket; it is a record of the family history.

Then there's the cherished grandfather clock, its steady tick a familiar tune in the family home. It stood in the hallway, marking the passage of time and witnessing countless family milestones. Handcrafted by a great-grandfather, it symbolizes his legacy of skill and hard work.

These heirlooms, each with their unique stories, illustrate the profound connections they create within families. The emotional significance of heirlooms lies in their ability to connect us to our roots and to remind us of the values and traditions that have been handed down through generations. They hold the power to evoke memories and transport us back to moments shared with those we loved. As you consider the future of your own family treasures, take the time to reflect on the stories they tell. Think about the hands that crafted them, the lives they've touched, and the legacy they represent. By thoughtfully selecting recipients and ensuring a fair distribution, you honor the past while paving the way for new stories to unfold.

Letters to Loved Ones: Your Final Goodbyes

Writing farewell letters allows you to articulate the thoughts and feelings that might otherwise remain unspoken. They offer a sense of closure, providing a final opportunity to express gratitude, love, and wishes for those who will carry on without you. Your words can provide a comforting embrace that wraps around your loved ones in moments when they need it the most. These letters hold the power to reassure and console, offering guidance and support when life's path becomes challenging. They become a legacy in themselves, a testament to the love and connections you've nurtured over a lifetime.

To write a meaningful letter, start by reflecting on the shared memories that define your relationship. Recall the laughter, challenges, and moments of growth that have strengthened your bond. Use these memories as a foundation to build your message, allowing them to guide your words and infuse your letter with authenticity. As you write, you may wish to offer words of wisdom—insights gained from your experiences that might serve as a beacon for your loved ones. Whether it's a lesson learned from a mistake or a principle that has guided your life, these nuggets of wisdom can provide direction and comfort long after you're gone.

The process of writing these letters is beneficial for the recipients and also for you. It can be a deeply healing exercise that offers a chance to reflect on your life, make peace with unresolved issues, and find solace in the knowledge that you've expressed your most heartfelt thoughts. For the writer, this act of expression can bring a sense of fulfillment, knowing that your words will live on as a source of strength and reassurance. For the recipients, receiving such a letter can provide emotional support, serving as a tangible reminder of your love and presence. It's a gift that continues to give, offering solace during difficult times and celebrating the connection that endures beyond physical separation.

To help you begin, consider using templates and prompts designed to spark inspiration and guide your writing. These tools can ease the initial hurdle of putting pen to paper, offering structure while allowing your personal voice to shine through. It may help to start your letter with a simple prompt, such as "One of my fondest memories with you is..." or "If I could offer one piece of advice, it would be...". These prompts encourage reflection and help you tap into the emotions and experiences that shape your relationship. Sample farewell letters can also provide a useful reference, illustrating various ways to express love, gratitude, and guidance. Use these examples as starting points then adapt and personalize them to suit your unique connections.

Writing these letters is an act of love and a way to ensure that your voice and presence remain with those you care about. It's a chance to leave behind a piece of yourself, a reminder that love transcends time and space. As you craft these messages, remember that the words you choose will serve as a lasting testament to your relationships, a legacy of love and wisdom for your loved ones to cherish. Don't worry about perfection; sincerity and connection are far more important as they allow you to create something that speaks from the heart and will resonate with those you leave behind.

As we wrap up this chapter on personal messages and legacies, think of it like putting the final stitch in a giant quilt of love, wisdom, and connection. Your letters, heirlooms, and family traditions all come together to showcase your values—and probably your excellent taste in quirky memorabilia. With these heartfelt messages in place, you've built a solid foundation for a future that honors the past while still leaving room for all the cool stuff that's yet to come.

Now that we've got the sentimental bits covered, it's time to turn our attention to the practicalities of organizing and storing your planner. You'll want to make sure your plans are easily accessible—because let's face it, the last thing you want is for your well-organized intentions to be buried under a pile of random papers or books you never read but intended to. Let's make sure your plans are secure and ready to go for those who will carry them forward!

Chapter 9

ORGANIZING AND STORING YOUR PLANNER

Your planner can be vulnerable to unexpected physical and digital challenges that may threaten its integrity. This chapter offers guidance on how to protect your planner, ensuring it remains functional and well-preserved. Taking the necessary precautions will help prevent potential damage and keep your planner in good condition.

Firstly, secure storage is paramount. Consider the risk of environmental factors, such as fires or floods, which could easily damage or destroy your physical documents. It would be devastating to lose years of thoughtful planning to a burst pipe or an unexpected blaze. This is where fireproof and waterproof safes come into play. According to *The New York Times' Wirecutter*, the Honeywell 1114 Lightweight Fire and Waterproof Chest is a top contender, boasting the ability to withstand fires up to 1,700°F for an hour and keep contents dry longer than its competitors. Weighing 42 pounds and with the footprint of a mini fridge, it provides ample protection without compromising convenience. Alternatively, a safety deposit box at your local bank offers security, ensuring your planner is shielded from home-based disasters. These boxes are typically located within a fortified vault, providing peace of mind that your documents are safe from environmental harm and unauthorized access.

In our increasingly digital world, it's equally important to consider secure digital storage solutions. Encrypted cloud storage services offer a robust way to protect your planner from cyber threats. Sync.com, for example, provides zero-knowledge encryption, meaning even the company cannot access your data, ensuring your information remains confidential. This level of security is necessary for personal, sensitive, or confidential data, safeguarding against unauthorized access. Password-protected digital files add another layer of defense, ensuring that even if someone were to access your storage, they would still require the correct password to view your files. These digital solutions provide security and convenience, allowing you to access your planner from anywhere, at any time, without the need to lug around physical documents.

While security is paramount, accessibility is equally important. You want your planner to be easy to retrieve when needed, whether for a spontaneous update or in an emergency. Communicating the storage location to trusted individuals ensures that your planner can be accessed by those you've designated, even if you're not around to provide instructions. You could use labels and clear markers to enhance visibility, making it straightforward for others to identify and access the planner quickly. This could be as simple as a note in your planner itself or a discreet label on the safe or digital folder where it's stored. Such measures might seem minor, yet they significantly reduce the stress and confusion that can arise in urgent situations.

> **Call to Action: Secure Storage Checklist**
>
> To help you organize and store your planner effectively, complete the checklist below to ensure you've considered all aspects of secure storage:
>
> - Choose a fireproof and waterproof safe that fits your needs.
> - Rent a safety deposit box for an additional layer of security.
> - Select an encrypted cloud storage service to protect your digital files.
> - Ensure all digital files are password-protected for added security.
> - Communicate the storage location to at least two trusted individuals.
> - Use labels and clear markers for easy identification and access.

By taking these steps, you're protecting your planner from physical and digital threats and ensuring it's easily accessible to those who need it. In doing so, you provide peace of mind, knowing your meticulous planning efforts are safe and ready for whenever they're required.

Paper vs. Digital: Deciding the Best Format

Choosing between a paper and digital format for your planner might seem as simple as deciding your morning coffee order, but it involves more nuanced considerations. Each format brings its own set of advantages and challenges. Paper planners, for instance, exude a certain charm and tangibility. They offer durability and ease of access—there's no need to remember passwords or worry about software updates. You can scribble a note in the margins or highlight important sections with a neon pen. Some find the act of writing by hand to be meditative, a tactile connection to their thoughts and plans. There's also the simplicity of flipping through pages, with everything laid out in front of you, immune to technological hiccups like crashes or power outages.

On the flip side, digital planners bring a different kind of flexibility and convenience. They allow for seamless integration with other digital tools, like calendars and email, offering a holistic view of your schedule and tasks. The ability to search through entries with a simple keyword or set automated reminders can be a game changer for those juggling multiple responsibilities. Digital planners are also inherently portable, existing in the cloud and accessible from any device, anywhere. This flexibility can be a boon for those who travel frequently or prefer the convenience of having their planner at their fingertips, without the extra weight of a physical book.

When deciding on the best format for your planner, think about how comfortable you are with technology—or whether you still prefer the sweet sound of pen scratching on paper like it's 1999. If you love the tactile joy of crossing things off with a pen and find technology more of a "necessary evil" than a helpful tool, a traditional paper planner is probably your best bet. But if your smartphone is practically glued to your hand and you thrive on digital efficiency (who needs a paper trail when you've got cloud storage?), then a digital planner might be your best friend. Don't forget to think about portability and accessibility. If you're constantly on the go, juggling a million things, a digital planner might be your superhero, always just a tap away. But if you prefer the feeling of holding something in your hands, with the permanence and stability of good ol' paper, then a paper planner might be your trusted sidekick. The choice is yours—whether you're living in the digital age or you're more of a "pen and paper for life" kind of person.

A hybrid approach, combining both paper and digital formats, offers a balanced solution for those who appreciate aspects of each. This method allows you to scan and digitize paper documents, creating a digital backup that can be accessed if the original is misplaced or damaged. Maintaining a backup system ensures that your information is preserved, regardless of the format. This dual approach provides the best of both worlds—the tactile satisfaction of a paper planner and the technological benefits of a digital one. It's like having a safety net, ensuring that your plans remain intact no matter the circumstances.

To aid in setting up your chosen format, you could try utilizing templates and tools tailored to each. For paper planners, printable templates can help organize your entries, offering structure and consistency. These templates can be customized to fit your specific needs, whether you're tracking appointments, financial goals, or personal reflections. For digital planners, a variety of digital organization apps are available. Google Calendar, for example, can seamlessly integrate with your email for managing events and reminders, while tools like Asana or Trello offer project management capabilities, allowing for detailed task tracking and collaboration. These digital tools enhance your planner's functionality, turning it into a dynamic resource that adapts to your evolving needs and preferences.

Ultimately, the choice between paper and digital—or a mix of both—should reflect your lifestyle, preferences, and goals. Whether you find solace in the pages of a leather-bound journal or the efficiency of a digital app, choose a format that complements your way of organizing and planning. Picking what works for you will give you the convenience of a system that supports you in capturing your thoughts, managing your time, and securing your legacy.

Sharing the Key: Who Needs Access?

Sharing the key to your planner ensures your most trusted confidants can step in when necessary, without overstepping boundaries or compromising your privacy. The importance of controlled access cannot be overstated. By limiting access to only a select few, you prevent unauthorized changes that could lead to confusion or misinterpretation of your wishes. Privacy and security are paramount, as your planner likely contains sensitive information that, if leaked or altered, could cause significant issues for you and your loved ones. Cultivate a sense of responsibility and trust with those you choose to share access with.

When deciding who should have access to your planner, trustworthiness and reliability should be your guiding criteria. These individuals should be people who have proven themselves dependable in other areas of your life. They should be able to manage the responsibilities that come with access to such personal information. It's not just about having someone who can be counted on to follow through, but also someone who understands the weight of the task and respects the need for discretion. They should be capable of acting in your best interest, making informed decisions if the need arises, and communicating effectively with other stakeholders involved in your planning.

Once you've identified the right individuals, the next step is to ensure they have the means to access the planner when needed. This might involve sharing access codes or physical keys if you're using a safe. For digital planners, you'll need to provide detailed instructions on how to access files or accounts. This includes walkthroughs for navigating any software or digital platforms you're using, ensuring that they feel comfortable and confident in their ability to access the planner efficiently. It's wise to conduct a run-through with them, addressing any questions or concerns they may have. This proactive approach will prevent confusion and reinforce your confidence in their ability to manage the task.

Emergencies can arise when the appointed primary contact is unavailable, making it critical to have a backup plan in place. Designating backup contacts ensures that there's always someone ready to step in, maintaining continuity and preventing delays. This backup should be someone equally trustworthy and informed about your wishes, ensuring a seamless transition of responsibility. Additionally, creating an emergency access protocol can further safeguard against unforeseen circumstances. This protocol should include clear instructions on how to proceed if the primary contact cannot be reached, detailing steps to verify the situation and activate the backup plan. Such measures minimize the potential for chaos, providing a structured response to emergencies.

Incorporating these elements into your planning process is like setting up a well-oiled machine that runs smoothly—even if you're not there to yell at it. It ensures your plans stay on track, even if you're off somewhere, hopefully relaxing and not micromanaging. By handing over the key to those you trust, you're building a personal support squad who can step in and make sure everything goes according to plan. This will protect your interests while giving your chosen ones the tools and confidence they need to execute your wishes with the precision of a well-rehearsed performance (no stage fright allowed). So, go ahead and create that network, and rest easy knowing your plans will be in good hands, even if you're not around to hover over them like a hawk.

Regular Updates: Keeping Your Planner Current

Life is nothing if not dynamic, a constant ebb and flow of changes that often take us by surprise. Whether it's a new addition to the family, a change of address, or a shift in financial circumstances, these events underscore the importance of keeping your planner up-to-date. Your planner is a living document that evolves with you, reflecting the many facets of your life. Regular updates ensure that your planner accurately represents your current situation, allowing it to serve its intended purpose. By reflecting changes in personal information, such as new contact details or marital status, you maintain a clear and accurate record that prevents confusion down the line. Similarly, keeping your financial and legal details current ensures your assets are managed according to your wishes and that any necessary legal documents are enforceable.

Establishing a schedule for reviewing and updating your planner can make this task more manageable. What about setting aside time each year for a comprehensive review of your planner, much like an annual check-up for your financial and legal health? This practice will allow you to assess what has changed over the past year and make any necessary adjustments. However, not all changes can wait for an annual review. Immediate updates are vital following major life events, such as a marriage, the birth of a child, a significant purchase, or a change in employment. These events often bring with them a host of new details that will need to be captured in your planner to ensure it remains an accurate reflection of your life.

In our busy lives, it's easy to let updates slip through the cracks. Utilizing tools and reminders can help ensure that updates are not overlooked. Digital reminders and calendar alerts can serve as gentle nudges, prompting you to review your planner at regular intervals. Whether you use a smartphone app or a digital calendar, these tools can integrate seamlessly into your routine, making it easier to stay on top of updates. Additionally, using checklists for update tracking can provide a structured approach to the process. A checklist can guide you through the key areas that need reviewing, ensuring that nothing is missed. This systematic approach simplifies the task and provides a sense of accomplishment as you tick off completed items.

Keeping the relevant parties in the loop about any changes is just as important as making those changes in the first place—because what's the point of updating your plans if no one knows about it? Notifying your family members and executors when something significant changes ensures they're not caught off guard, trying to figure out why you suddenly want to be buried in a chicken suit. Open communication builds trust and keeps everything running smoothly, so there's less chance of your family arguing over whether you meant to leave your collection of vintage spoons to your cousin or your neighbor. Keeping a log of updates also helps—think of it as your own personal "history of decisions," so everyone can see exactly why you did what you did, without having to guess. Whether it's a simple document in your planner or a separate file, this log ensures that anyone involved in executing your wishes can easily follow the trail of your genius decision-making.

By maintaining regular updates, you create a planner that is a reliable resource and a reflection of your life as it is now. This practice will ensure that your planner remains relevant and effective, ready to support you and your loved ones in times of need. It also reinforces the importance of adaptability, reminding us that while change is inevitable, our response to it can be thoughtfully managed.

With these strategies in place, your planner will become more than just a collection of notes and instructions. It will evolve into a testament to your foresight and care, a well-maintained guide that captures the essence of your life and paves the way for a smoother future. As you move forward, let these updates serve as reminders of the importance of staying engaged with your planning efforts, ensuring that your legacy is one of clarity, intention, and love.

In the following chapter, we'll explore the final elements of preparing your planner, reinforcing its value in ensuring your wishes are honored and your loved ones are supported.

Chapter 10

Ensuring Implementation and Family Engagement

When discussing estate planning, one important consideration is choosing the right executor to manage your affairs after your passing. The executor is responsible for ensuring that your wishes, as outlined in your will, are carried out effectively. This includes handling tasks such as distributing assets, paying debts, and managing any legal or financial responsibilities. You need to select someone who is organized, responsible, and able to make decisions calmly and thoughtfully. An executor should be capable of navigating the complexities of estate administration without becoming overwhelmed by the process.

An executor's role is multifaceted. They manage and distribute assets, ensuring that everything from bank accounts to heirlooms finds its rightful owner. This responsibility extends to filing necessary legal documents, a task that requires attention to detail and a methodical approach. The executor also acts as the bridge between your estate and its beneficiaries, communicating with them to clarify roles, timelines, and any questions that might arise. It's a position that demands a blend of organizational prowess, financial acumen, and a knack for diplomacy, especially when emotions run high.

When selecting an executor, consider criteria that go beyond family ties or friendships. Look for someone with financial acumen and organizational skills, as they'll be tasked with managing complex assets and adhering to timelines. The ability to remain impartial is equally vital—debates over who gets what can be fraught, and you'll want someone who can handle this without favoritism. According to Kiplinger, it's wise to avoid naming executors who have conflicts with beneficiaries, as this could lead to disputes that hinder the process. An executor should be patient and emotionally grounded, able to endure the potentially lengthy and frustrating probate process with grace.

Being an executor can be a real test of character—because managing family drama and complex estates is no small feat. Imagine trying to break up a fight between siblings over who gets the family heirloom, all while keeping a straight face and not muttering, "I told you so!" Emotions can run high when legacies are at stake, so handling disputes requires a delicate touch. Managing complex estates can also get tricky, especially when there are a bunch of assets or financial arrangements that could make even the most seasoned accountant break a sweat. To make life easier for your poor executor, give them clear instructions and resources that spell out exactly what you want. And don't forget about the legal experts—because no one wants to be stuck Googling "how to handle estate taxes" at the last minute. By providing your executor with the right tools and guidance, you're setting them up for success, so they can handle your estate with the kind of care and precision that would make even Martha Stewart proud.

Family Meetings: Sharing Your Plans

Family meetings hold the power to transform complex estate plans into understandable, shared commitments. They offer a space where everyone can gather to discuss important matters, ensuring that the air is clear and confusion is left at the door. By encouraging open dialogue, you can cultivate an environment where roles and expectations are well communicated and understood. This is especially important when discussing sensitive issues, as it allows each family member to voice concerns or ask questions in a supportive setting. Clarifying these roles upfront can prevent misunderstandings later, making the process smoother for everyone involved.

To make these meetings effective, careful preparation is necessary. Start by setting a clear agenda. This keeps the discussion focused and ensures that all important topics are addressed. Encourage active participation from all family members by inviting them to share their thoughts and concerns. This engagement can be facilitated by assigning specific topics to different people, allowing each individual to contribute to the conversation. The goal is to create a collaborative atmosphere where everyone feels valued and heard. When family members are actively involved in discussions, they are more likely to feel invested in the outcomes, making the implementation of your plans more seamless.

During these meetings, a few key topics should definitely take center stage—preferably with some dramatic music in the background for added effect. First up: your after-death planner. This review ensures everyone is on the same page, and they're not left guessing whether you really want your ashes scattered in the backyard or at that weird roadside diner you loved. Next, discuss each person's responsibilities, making sure everyone knows exactly what's expected of them when the time comes. These conversations help clear up any confusion and ease anxiety. Finally, addressing these roles in a group setting makes it clear that no one is in this alone—it's a team effort, and everyone has their part to play, even if that part involves organizing all those old photos no one knows what to do with.

Discussing sensitive topics requires a gentle touch. Try to address emotional concerns with empathy, acknowledging that the subject matter can be difficult for some. Allow space for emotions to be expressed, while gently steering the conversation back to the practical matters at hand. Maintaining a supportive environment encourages honesty and openness, which are essential for productive discussions. To help manage these conversations, you may wish to lay some ground rules, such as listening without interrupting and keeping the dialogue respectful. By creating a respectful atmosphere, you create a safe space where important but difficult topics can be discussed with care and consideration.

Handling Resistance: When Family Disagrees

Resistance to estate plans can often bubble up from deep and varied sources. Sometimes, it's as simple as differences in personal values. Perhaps one family member values tradition and expects assets to be distributed in a way that reflects it, while another might prioritize financial necessity or egalitarian principles. Misunderstandings or lack of information can also stoke the fires of disagreement. Without clear communication, assumptions take root, leading to misguided conclusions about intentions and decisions. These misunderstandings can fracture discussions, as family members may feel left in the dark or unfairly treated. You must recognize that these feelings, though challenging, are common and can be handled well with care and attention.

Addressing and overcoming these disagreements requires a strategy. Facilitated mediation can be a powerful tool, bringing in a neutral third party to guide the conversation and help untangle emotional knots. This mediator can provide perspective, ensuring that all voices are heard and respected. Open and honest communication remains the cornerstone of resolving conflicts. It's about creating a space where family members feel safe to express their thoughts and concerns without fear of backlash. Encouraging transparency and vulnerability can lead to breakthroughs, fostering understanding and empathy. An environment of honesty can bridge gaps and mend rifts that might otherwise grow into chasms.

Compromise is often the secret ingredient in these family matters—it's like the duct tape that holds everything together when things get a little too "colorful." Finding middle ground doesn't mean everyone gets exactly what they want, but it does mean that everyone feels like their concerns have been heard, even if that means Aunt Susan doesn't get to keep *all* the vintage holiday decorations. Negotiating solutions that everyone can live with can turn a full-blown family feud into a collaborative effort—kind of like turning a food fight into a potluck dinner. Maybe one sibling agrees to take on more responsibility in exchange for a bigger piece of the estate pie, or perhaps a prized heirloom gets passed around like a cherished family trophy. These compromises require a little flexibility and the ability to see beyond your own "I deserve that!" moment and focus on the family's greater good. Ultimately, successful conflict resolution is all about prioritizing collective harmony over individual gain, because no one wants to be the one who gets stuck with all the paperwork—or the awkward silence at the next family gathering.

Examples of families who have navigated these turbulent waters can offer hope and guidance. Take the case of the Cooper's, who faced a heated debate over their late mother's art collection. Through mediation, they found a way to divide the pieces that honored their mother's wishes while respecting each sibling's personal connection to the art. In another scenario, the Alvarez family learned that by holding regular family discussions, they could address misunderstandings before they escalated into disputes. These stories illustrate that while conflicts are inevitable, they are not insurmountable. With patience, empathy, and a commitment to unity, families can emerge from disagreements stronger and more cohesive.

Bridging the Generation Gap: Engaging Younger Family Members

Involving younger family members in estate planning is more than a nod to the future—it's a bridge that connects generations, ensuring the continuity of knowledge and traditions. Young adults often bring fresh perspectives, digital savvy, and a willingness to embrace change that can invigorate family discussions about planning. By engaging them, you're not only transferring vital knowledge but also instilling a sense of responsibility and involvement in family affairs. This engagement fosters a deeper understanding of family values and creates a shared commitment to preserving them. Encouraging younger members to participate in decision-making allows them to feel valued and respected, and it ensures that the family's evolving dynamics are reflected in the plans.

To capture the interest of younger generations, incorporate digital tools and apps into the planning process. Platforms like Trello or Asana can make organizing tasks interactive and collaborative, while apps focused on financial planning can provide insights that resonate with tech-savvy individuals. Involving them in discussions about digital estate planning, such as managing social media accounts and digital assets, can also highlight the relevance of the process in today's world. By integrating these tools, you not only make the planning process more accessible but also actively engage younger members in a way that aligns with their interests and skills.

Engaging younger family members in estate planning can feel like trying to convince a cat to take a bath—it's not impossible, but it sure has its challenges. The main issue? Communication styles. Younger generations are all about texting, emojis, and quick replies—forget about sitting down for a serious face-to-face discussion. Meanwhile, you're over here, ready to pull out the old family photo albums for a nostalgic chat. Add to that the varying levels of interest in estate planning (because, let's face it, not everyone is as excited about wills and taxes as we are), and it's easy to see why they might check out. But don't worry, there's hope! To bridge the gap, meet them where they are. Encourage casual, no-pressure conversations where they can ask questions and share their thoughts—preferably without making it feel like a pop quiz. And, with a little creativity, you can transform what seems like a dry, "fun-free" topic into something that feels relevant, interesting, and maybe even a little exciting. Who knew estate planning could become the next big family bonding activity?

Consider families who have successfully involved younger members. One family turned their estate planning into a project, inviting their teenage children to create a digital family history, complete with interviews and archived photos. Not only did this task teach the younger generation about their heritage, but it also sparked an interest in family traditions. In another family, the youngest members took charge of a sustainability initiative, ensuring the family's values of conservation were woven into the estate plans. These examples show that engagement doesn't have to follow a set script; it can be as creative and varied as the families themselves.

Reviewing and Revising: Keeping Your Plans Relevant

In the ever-changing landscape of life, regular reviews of your plans ensure they stay relevant and effective. As time passes, life is bound to bring changes—new family members, career shifts, or even a move to a new city. Each change can alter the dynamics of your estate plans, making it crucial to revisit them regularly. This reflection allows you to update legal and financial information, ensuring your plans continue to reflect your current circumstances and intentions. Imagine discovering that a beneficiary has moved or changed their name—these are simple updates, yet they can prevent future confusion.

Setting a schedule for revising your plans is like setting a reminder to clean out your email inbox—because if you don't, things can quickly spiral out of control. Annual reviews are your built-in "check-up," giving you a chance to tweak things before they become overwhelming. Life throws enough curveballs as it is, so it helps to know when it's time to update your plans—like when you get married, have a baby, or suddenly realize your financial situation has changed because you bought way too many online gadgets. These milestones bring new things to consider, like "Who gets the house?" or "Who gets the pet goldfish?" By establishing a regular routine for revising, you keep your plans in sync with your ever-evolving life. Plus, it's way less stressful than scrambling to update everything in one massive panic when life hands you a big change.

Approaching revisions systematically can ease the process. Checklists serve as valuable tools, guiding you through each aspect of your plans and highlighting areas that might need attention. Involving family members can provide additional insights, ensuring that your plans align with both your wishes and the evolving family dynamics. Their input can shed light on potential blind spots, offering perspectives that enhance the comprehensiveness of your plans. This collaboration not only strengthens the plans but also fosters a sense of collective responsibility and investment among family members.

Professional advisors play a vital role in this process, offering expertise that can refine and enhance your plans. Legal and financial advisors provide valuable guidance, ensuring that your plans adhere to current laws and best practices. Estate planners can offer strategic insights, suggesting adjustments that maximize the effectiveness of your plans. Their expertise ensures that your plans are not only legally sound but also optimized to achieve your goals. By consulting these professionals during revisions, you harness their knowledge to create plans that are robust and resilient.

Legal Review: Ensuring Compliance

Legal compliance in estate planning is about laying a solid foundation that withstands the test of time and scrutiny. By ensuring that your plans meet legal requirements, you effectively shield your estate from potential disputes and challenges that can arise when things aren't crystal clear. This clarity is crucial because it ensures your wishes are enforceable, reducing the likelihood of disagreements among beneficiaries or delays in executing your plans. Without this, even the most carefully crafted intentions can unravel, leaving your loved ones in a tangle of uncertainty and legal red tape—an outcome no one desires during an already challenging time.

Conducting a thorough legal review requires a keen eye for detail and an understanding of what to prioritize. Start by checking for outdated documents. Laws change, and so do personal circumstances; a will or trust drafted a decade ago might not reflect current realities or legal standards. Ensuring alignment with current laws is another critical step. This might involve reviewing changes in tax laws or inheritance regulations that could impact your estate. A legal review acts like a tune-up for your estate plan, keeping it running smoothly and efficiently through life's inevitable twists and turns.

Legal professionals play a pivotal role in this process, offering the expertise needed to navigate the complex legal landscape. They provide invaluable advice and updates, keeping you informed about changes that might affect your plans. Drafting and revising legal documents is their forte, ensuring that every detail is meticulously attended to. Their involvement brings a level of precision and assurance that laypersons often cannot achieve alone. Choosing the right legal advisor is a decision that should be made with care. Evaluate their credentials and experience, seeking recommendations from trusted sources to find someone who is both knowledgeable and trustworthy. This relationship is foundational, offering you peace of mind as you entrust them with safeguarding your legacy.

Feedback and Improvement: Learning from Your Family's Input

Incorporating family feedback into your planning process can substantially enhance the effectiveness of your estate plans. When you invite family members to share their thoughts, you gain access to a wealth of insights that might otherwise be overlooked. This feedback serves as a valuable tool for identifying potential issues or oversights in your plans. Family members often bring diverse perspectives, offering fresh ideas or pointing out areas that need refinement. Their input can reveal hidden concerns or preferences that you might not have considered, ensuring that your plans are comprehensive and balanced.

To effectively gather feedback, consider using structured methods like surveys or questionnaires. These tools allow family members to express their thoughts in a considered manner, free from the pressures of group discussions. Alternatively, you might hold feedback sessions during family meetings, where everyone can openly discuss their views. These sessions foster an environment of collaboration, where ideas are shared and debated constructively. It's important to create a space where all voices are heard, ensuring that feedback is both honest and respectful.

> ### Call to Action: Create a Survey for Your Family Members
>
> Here's a lighthearted yet practical quiz you can give your family members to get a sense of who would prefer what items when you're gone. It's a fun way to get the conversation started and ensure your belongings end up where they'll be appreciated (or at least enjoyed with some thoughtfulness.)

Welcome to the *"What Would You Like to Inherit?"* Quiz!

This fun little questionnaire helps me understand which of my treasured possessions would be most loved by which family members. Answer the questions, and remember—no hard feelings! The goal is to make sure everything goes where it will be appreciated!

Which item do you secretly covet the most in my home?
A. My vintage collection of teacups
B. The giant painting of my cat
C. My collection of odd, quirky souvenirs from travel
D. The leather-bound books I never actually read but look impressive
E. Anything else that has sentimental value (but definitely NOT my cat painting)

How would you feel about taking over the responsibility of my plants?
A. I'm a plant whisperer—I'll keep them alive and thriving!
B. I'll water them twice a month and hope for the best.
C. I'll probably kill them all, but I'm willing to try!
D. No thanks—I'll just take the picture of the plant instead.

Which of these family heirlooms do you think should be passed down to you?
A. The old family cookbook (I can handle all those weird recipes)
B. The silverware set that's been in the family for centuries
C. The antique rocking chair that's as creaky as my knees
D. The photo album, so I can understand what kind of chaos you inherited

What would you prefer to inherit from my wardrobe?
A. That super stylish coat I've worn maybe once
B. The vintage scarves that I keep "just in case"
C. The "I'm going to wear this to a fancy event" clothes I never actually wear
D. The comfy socks—because let's face it, who doesn't need extra comfy socks?

If I have a secret stash of candy (or snacks) hidden somewhere, who's most likely to find it?
A. You know I've got a sixth sense for snacks.
B. I'll hunt it down like a treasure hunt.
C. Maybe... I'll pretend I didn't know it was there.
D. I'm not really a candy person, but thanks for the thought.

Which of these would you be willing to "safely store" for future generations (even if you never actually use it)?
A. My collection of thimbles
B. That giant pile of sentimental letters from friends
C. My collection of vintage kitchen gadgets that *might* be useful one day
D. My high school yearbook—because who doesn't love a trip down memory lane?

How do you feel about receiving a family tradition or ritual to carry on?
A. Love it! I'm ready to take on the family duties with pride.
B. Sure, I'll try—if it's not too complicated.
C. Not sure what I'm getting into, but I'll give it a shot.
D. I'd rather just remember the tradition than have to keep it going.

Scoring:

- Mostly A's: You're ready to take it all on! Your heart is in the right place and you're definitely ready to handle all the family treasures (and plants).

- Mostly B's: You'll give it your best shot, but some things might need a little extra TLC.

- Mostly C's: You're a bit hesitant, but you're open to taking on some of the legacy with a little help (or maybe just a gentle nudge).

- Mostly D's: You're here for the memories, but don't worry too much about the heirlooms—just promise you'll cherish the stories.

Feel free to pass this quiz around at the next family gathering, and don't be surprised if it turns into a lively conversation about who *really* deserves the cat painting. Change the questions to fit your style and belongings. It'll be a fun way to start planning for the future while keeping things lighthearted.

Once you've collected feedback, the challenge lies in implementing it effectively. Start by prioritizing actionable feedback, focusing on suggestions that align with your overall goals. Balance individual preferences with these goals to ensure that the plans remain cohesive and focused. Not every piece of feedback will be feasible, but by integrating the most relevant suggestions, you demonstrate a commitment to considering your family's needs. This approach not only improves the plans but also strengthens family bonds, as members see their contributions valued and respected.

Continuous improvement is the key to keeping your plans relevant and effective over time. Life is dynamic, and your plans should be too. By regularly revisiting and refining your plans with family input, you ensure they evolve in step with changing circumstances. This ongoing process builds stronger family relationships, as it fosters a culture of openness and collaboration. It also reinforces the idea that estate planning is not just a one-time task but an ongoing dialogue, adapting and growing with your family's needs and values.

Celebrating Life: Planning a Living Memorial

Imagine celebrating life while living. A living memorial is just that—a vibrant tribute to your life's journey, shared with loved ones. It's about creating lasting memories before the final farewell. Rather than waiting for others to gather in your absence, take charge and celebrate your life with those who matter most. Organize a family reunion or gathering, a chance to bring everyone together in a spirit of joy and reflection. It's not only an opportunity to laugh and reminisce but also to solidify connections that span generations. Consider a legacy project or charity, something that reflects your values and passions, ensuring your impact continues long after you're gone.

The emotional benefits of a living memorial are like the ultimate family reunion—minus the awkward "who's sitting next to who?" drama. These celebrations strengthen family bonds by giving everyone a chance to share stories, laugh about the good times, and maybe even admit that Uncle Bob *was* right about the gravy recipe. It's a time for gratitude to flow, where everyone can focus on the positive and remember the joyful moments rather than dwelling on the sad ones. As stories are swapped and memories relived, you'll feel a sense of closure, like that moment when you find the last piece of a puzzle you've been working on forever. It gives everyone peace of mind and a deeper understanding of your legacy—basically, a family therapy session without the therapist. These celebrations offer a chance to openly express love and gratitude, free from the weight of grief. Plus, they leave a lasting impression, offering a tangible reminder of the joy, laughter, and love that make your life so unforgettable. And let's face it—who doesn't want to be remembered for making the best potato salad ever?

Consider examples of successful living memorials. One family turned their patriarch's passion for gardening into a community project, planting a garden that continues to bloom year after year. Not only did it beautify the neighborhood, but it also became a place for family gatherings where they could remember their loved one through shared work and enjoyment. Another family created a scholarship fund in honor of a beloved teacher, celebrating their dedication to education by supporting future generations. These unique memorials not only honor the individual but also inspire and uplift those involved, transforming the concept of a memorial into a celebration of life and legacy.

Finding Peace: Letting Go and Moving On

Embracing the inevitability of change is a profound aspect of life, especially when it involves planning for the end. This process often stirs deep emotions, as it requires confronting one's mortality and the impact of one's absence on loved ones. Yet, it also offers a unique opportunity to reflect on the legacy you will leave behind. Finding peace in this context means accepting that change is a constant, and that by planning thoughtfully, you can ensure your values and wishes continue to resonate. Letting go doesn't mean forgetting; rather, it allows you to focus on the meaningful connections and memories you've created.

To support the emotional journey of letting go, consider integrating mindfulness and self-care into your routine. Mindfulness encourages you to stay present, acknowledging emotions without judgment, which can help ease anxiety about the future. Self-care, on the other hand, involves nurturing your physical and emotional well-being through activities that bring joy and relaxation. Whether it's a walk in nature, meditation, or enjoying a favorite hobby, these practices create a foundation of inner strength and resilience. Seeking support from loved ones is equally important; sharing your thoughts and feelings with those you trust can provide comfort and reinforce bonds.

Closure plays a vital role in achieving a sense of fulfillment. Taking time to reflect on your life achievements can instill pride and contentment, highlighting the positive impact you've made. Expressing gratitude to those who have shared your journey adds depth to these reflections, fostering a sense of completion. Forgiveness, whether extended to others or yourself, releases lingering regrets, making room for peace. Together, these practices form a tapestry of emotional healing, guiding you toward a tranquil acceptance of what lies ahead.

To make this process a little less overwhelming, consider tapping into resources like therapists who specialize in grief (because sometimes you just need someone to listen to you rant about how your favorite socks are missing), support groups where you can bond with others who truly get it, and professionals who can offer gentle guidance without making you feel like you're in an episode of a courtroom drama. Books that explore themes of change and acceptance can also help you gain some perspective—because nothing says "comfort" like curling up with a book that tells you it's okay to cry, laugh, and eat an entire pint of ice cream in one sitting. With these tools and insights in hand, you'll be able to embrace the legacy you leave behind with confidence, knowing it reflects the richness of your experiences and all the wisdom you've collected along the way.

Conclusion

As you reach the final pages of this book, take a moment to pat yourself on the back for making it this far—and for planning ahead like a true life strategist. Let's face it, thinking about what happens after we leave this world isn't exactly the most thrilling dinner conversation, but it's one of the most considerate things you can do for your loved ones. It's all about keeping the family drama to a minimum (because no one wants a soap opera after you're gone), providing clarity when emotions run high, and offering peace of mind when life throws its toughest curveballs. Throughout these chapters, we've explored how a little thoughtful planning can prevent disputes, lighten emotional loads, and ensure your legacy lives on without anyone fighting over who gets the vintage lamp. So, congratulations on tackling this important, yet often avoided, task. You've officially secured your spot as the family's most prepared member—right next to the person who keeps their pantry stocked with emergency snacks.

We've covered a lot of ground together. From setting the stage for peace by understanding the importance of planning ahead, to diving into personal information essentials and financial organization, each section aimed to equip you with the knowledge and tools necessary for effective after-death planning. We ventured into the digital realm to manage your online legacy, discussed healthcare directives, and explored the nuances of funeral and burial preferences. Each chapter offered insights and practical advice, designed to guide you step-by-step through this impactful process.

One of the key takeaways from this book is the importance of being proactive. We've provided interactive elements such as checklists, templates, and reflective prompts to facilitate your planning journey. These tools are here to help you take action, whether you're starting from scratch or refining existing plans. By utilizing these resources, you can transform what might seem like an overwhelming task into a manageable and even rewarding endeavor.

Throughout this book, we've woven humor into the fabric of serious topics. By lightening the mood, we aimed to make conversations about death more approachable and less intimidating. Humor allows us to break down barriers and open up essential dialogues, helping us connect with our loved ones in meaningful ways. Consider including a funny family story or crafting a light-hearted epitaph—these touches can make the planning process a little less daunting and a lot more personal.

Your initiative to plan for the future showcases a remarkable blend of emotional courage and responsibility. It's not an easy task, but the effort you put forth today will ease the path for your family tomorrow. I'm grateful for your trust and commitment, and I hope this book has been a valuable companion in your planning process.

As you move forward, I encourage you to share your experiences and insights with others. By fostering a community of informed and proactive planners, we can collectively pave the way for more harmonious family transitions. Share your journey, your stories, and the lessons you've learned. In doing so, you help others recognize the importance of planning, making a difference beyond your own circle.

Take a moment to reflect on your personal motivations. Consider the impact your planning efforts will have on your loved ones. This is more than just a practical exercise; it's a profound expression of love and care. By preparing for the inevitable, you're ensuring that your legacy is one of thoughtfulness and grace.

As you continue this journey, remember that support is always within reach. There are numerous resources available to help you implement your plans. Online forums, additional reading materials, and communities of like-minded individuals can provide guidance and encouragement. You're not alone in this process, and the support you seek will reinforce the planning efforts you have undertaken.

In closing, I hope this book has inspired you to take control of your end-of-life planning. Embrace the tools and insights provided, and use them to create a plan that reflects your values and wishes. Your legacy is a testament to the life you've lived, and your thoughtful planning will ensure it continues to shine brightly for those you leave behind. Thank you for allowing me to be part of this important journey with you.

Dear Readers,

Thank you for taking the time to explore **The Ultimate End of Life Planner** *and for allowing me to be a part of your journey in planning and organizing the important aspects of life.* Your support and encouragement mean the world to me.

I hope this book has provided clarity, comfort, and actionable steps to help you plan for the future, ensuring peace of mind for yourself and your loved ones. If you found value in its pages, I would greatly appreciate it if you could take a few moments to leave a review.

Your feedback not only helps others discover this book but also allows me to continue creating resources that empower and guide people through life's important transitions. Whether it's a brief comment on what resonated most with you or a detailed reflection on how the book has impacted your planning, your words will make a difference..

To share your review please scan the QR code or visit the link below.

https://www.amazon.com/review/review-your-purchases/?asin=B0DTV456KS

Thank you for being a part of this mission to foster thoughtful preparation and meaningful connections.

With gratitude,
Nicole Reap

Glossary

1. **Appraiser** – A professional who estimates the value of assets, such as property or personal belongings.

2. **Assets** – Items of value owned by an individual, such as money, property, or investments.

3. **Audit** – A detailed review of financial records to ensure accuracy and compliance.

4. **Beneficiary** – A person or entity designated to receive assets from a will, trust, or insurance policy.

5. **Burial** – The act of placing a deceased person's body in the ground as part of the final rites.

6. **Cloud** – A system for storing and accessing data remotely over the internet, rather than on local devices.

7. **Cremation** – The process of reducing a body to ashes through heat and flame, typically as an alternative to burial.

8. **Cybercriminal** – An individual who engages in illegal activities online, such as identity theft or fraud.

9. **Digital assets** – Electronic items of value, including photos, documents, and online accounts.

10. **Digital footprint** – The trail of data left by a person's online activities, such as social media and browsing history.

11. **Digital storage** – The method of saving data on electronic devices or cloud platforms.

12. **Digital vault** – A secure online storage service for protecting sensitive digital assets like passwords and documents.

13. **Do Not Resuscitate (DNR)** – A medical order indicating that a person does not want to be revived if they stop breathing or their heart stops.

14. **Embalming** – The process of preserving a body to delay decomposition, often for viewing at a funeral.

15. **Epitaph** – A short text or inscription in memory of someone, typically placed on a tombstone.

16. **Estate** – The total assets and property owned by an individual at the time of their death.

17. **Executor** – The person appointed to carry out the instructions in a will and manage the estate after death.

18. **Family tree** – A visual representation or diagram showing the ancestry and descendants of an individual.

19. **Funeral** – A ceremony held to honor and remember a deceased person, often involving a burial or cremation.

20. **Green burials** – An environmentally friendly burial method that avoids embalming and uses biodegradable materials.

21. **Grief** – The intense sorrow or sadness experienced after the death of a loved one.

22. **Heirlooms** – Valuable or sentimental items passed down through generations within a family.

23. **Legacy** – The impact, wealth, or values passed down from one generation to another, often through a will or trust.

24. **Life insurance** – A contract that provides a financial payout to beneficiaries upon the policyholder's death.

25. **Living will** – A legal document that outlines a person's wishes regarding medical treatment if they become unable to communicate.

26. **Mediator** – A neutral third party who helps resolve disputes or conflicts, often in legal or family matters.

27. **Memorial service** – A ceremony or gathering held to remember and celebrate the life of someone who has passed away.

28. **Net worth** – The total value of an individual's assets minus liabilities, indicating their financial standing.

29. **Obituary** – A published notice of someone's death, typically including details of their life and funeral arrangements.

30. **Palliative care** – Medical care focused on providing relief from the symptoms of serious illness, rather than curing it.

31. **Password** – A secret word or code used to access secure information or accounts.

32. **Persistent vegetative state** – A condition in which a person is awake but not aware or responsive, typically following a severe brain injury.

33. **Power of Attorney** – A legal document granting someone the authority to act on another person's behalf in financial or medical matters.

34. **Real estate** – Property consisting of land and the buildings on it, as well as natural resources.

35. **Social media** – Websites and platforms where individuals can share content, communicate, and interact online.

36. **Terminal illness** – A disease or condition that is expected to result in death within a short period of time.

37. **Title deed** – A legal document that proves ownership of a property or land.

38. **Trust** – A legal arrangement where one person holds assets for the benefit of another, managed by a trustee.

39. **Will** – A legal document that outlines a person's wishes regarding the distribution of their assets after death.

About the Author

NICOLE REAP is a passionate educator, seasoned entrepreneur, and acclaimed author dedicated to empowering others with essential life skills. Nicole has spent decades teaching, writing, and mentoring individuals of all ages. She aims to simplify complex topics, making them accessible and practical for everyday life.

Nicole's literary journey includes works such as *Vagus Nerve Vitality*, *Somatic Therapy for Beginners*, and *Money Skills for Teens Made Easy*. Each book reflects her commitment to fostering personal growth, healing, and financial literacy.

Her latest book, *The Ultimate End-of-Life Planning Guide,* tackles the often-overlooked topic of end-of-life planning with compassion and clarity. Inspired by her personal experiences managing her late mother's and grandparents' affairs, Nicole offers readers a thoughtful guide to organizing personal items, financial assets, and posthumous wishes. The book is both a practical resource and a heartfelt companion for those navigating life's final chapter.

When she's not writing or teaching preschool, Nicole enjoys exploring nature, RV adventures, ocean wildlife, golfing, and spending time with her two daughters and loyal canine companions. She lives in Maryland, where her love for learning, teaching, and family inspires her work.

For more information about Nicole and her books, visit:
https://www.nicolereap.com

REFERENCES

Why Is Estate Planning Important?
https://www.usbank.com/financialiq/plan-your-future/trusts-and-estates/why-estate-planning-is-important.html

Make 'Em Laugh: How Humor Can Be the Secret Weapon in ...
https://www.gsb.stanford.edu/insights/make-em-laugh-how-humor-can-be-secret-weapon-your-communication

Comprehensive Guide to Digital Estate Planning: Secure ...
https://bluenotary.us/digital-estate-planning/

How to Talk to Loved Ones About End-of-Life Plans
https://www.betterplaceforests.com/blog/how-to-talk-to-loved-ones-about-end-of-life-plans-8/

101 Data Protection Tips: How to Protect Your Data
https://www.digitalguardian.com/blog/101-data-protection-tips-how-keep-your-passwords-financial-personal-information-online-safe

Identity Document Verification: What is it and How Does ...
https://microblink.com/resources/blog/documentation-verification/

12 Best Family Tree Software & Tools for 2024 - Venngage
https://venngage.com/blog/best-family-tree-software/

Choosing an Emergency Contact -- It Matters
https://www.nolo.com/legal-encyclopedia/your-emergency-contact-it-matters.html

CHECKLIST: 5 Steps to Organize Your Finances
https://www.sdtplanning.com/organize-your-finances-checklist

Best Online Brokers and Trading Platforms for November ...
https://www.investopedia.com/best-online-brokers-4587872

10 Uses of Life Insurance in Estate Planning
https://www.ameritas.com/insights/10-uses-of-life-insurance-in-estate-planning/

Estate Planning With A Large Amount of Debt
https://jgcg.com/how-to-handle-your-estate-planning-when-a-large-amount-of-debt-is-involved/

Digital Legacy: how to organise your online life for after you ...
https://www.theguardian.com/money/2023/oct/16/how-to-manage-digital-legacy-after-death-will

Request to Memorialize or Remove an Account - Facebook
https://www.facebook.com/help/1111566045566400

The Best Password Managers for 2024
https://www.pcmag.com/picks/the-best-password-managers

5 digital vaults: Pros, cons, and which is right for you
https://www.freewill.com/learn/comparing-digital-vault-platforms/

Living wills and advance directives for medical decisions
https://www.mayoclinic.org/healthy-lifestyle/consumer-health/in-depth/living-wills/art-20046303#:~:text=By%20planning%20ahead%2C%20you%20can,to%20make%20on%20your%20behalf.

Power of Attorney Laws: 50-State Survey
https://www.justia.com/estate-planning/power-of-attorney/power-of-attorney-laws-50-state-survey/

How To Make a Living Will | MetLife
https://www.metlife.com/stories/legal/how-to-make-a-living-will/

Advance directive vs. living will: What's the difference?
https://www.freewill.com/learn/advance-directive-vs-living-will

Funeral Planning Checklist: Considerations for Families
https://www.homesteaderslife.com/blog/funeral-planning-checklist-considerations-for-families

Environmental impacts of funerals: burial vs cremation - Bare
https://bare.com.au/blog/environmental-impacts-of-funerals-death-burial-vs-cremation

Imaginative Ways to Personalize Your Loved One's Funeral
https://www.griecofunerals.com/ways-to-personalize-your-loved-ones-funeral

Having the Last Word: How to Write Your Own Obituary
https://www.aarp.org/home-family/friends-family/info-2023/how-to-write-your-own-obituary.html

Drafting an Estate Inventory for Estate Planning or Probate
https://nestegg.cloud/blog/estate-inventory-for-estate-planning-or-probate/

Why Title Deeds are Important - Sanchez | Medina Law Group
https://www.sanchez-medina.com/post/why-title-deeds-are-important

Find an Appraiser https://aiohio.org/appraiser.php

Fair or Equal: Which is Right for Your Estate Plan?
https://www.1834.com/insights/fair-or-equal-which-is-right-for-your-estate-plan/

Leaving a Message After Death
https://www.betterplaceforests.com/blog/leaving-a-message-after-death/

The Importance of Family Traditions and Rituals
https://www.theelefant.com/blogs/the-importance-of-family-traditions-and-rituals

5 steps to protect family heirlooms
https://www.legalzoom.com/articles/5-steps-to-protect-family-heirlooms

FREE Goodbye Letter Templates - Download in Word, ...
https://www.template.net/letters/goodbye

The 4 Best Fireproof Document Safes of 2024
https://www.nytimes.com/wirecutter/reviews/best-fireproof-document-safe/

Best Encrypted Cloud Storage in 2024 [Secure Online File ...
https://www.cloudwards.net/best-encrypted-cloud-storage/

15 Best Digital Organization Tools
https://www.katheats.com/best-digital-organization-tools

SEC03-BP03 Establish emergency access process
https://docs.aws.amazon.com/wellarchitected/latest/framework/sec_permissions_emergency_process.html

7 *Tips for Choosing the Right Executor*
https://www.kiplinger.com/article/retirement/t021-c032-s014-7-tips-for-choosing-the-right-executor.html

How to Have a Productive Family Meeting About Estate ...
https://elisebuiefamilylaw.com/how-to-have-a-productive-family-meeting-about-estate-planning/

Resolving Family Inheritance Disputes: Explore Options
https://www.giambronelaw.com/site/advice/dispute-resolution/family-disputes/resolving-family-inheritance-disputes/

Six Estate Planning Tips for Younger Generations
https://www.kiplinger.com/retirement/estate-planning-tips-for-younger-generations

Printed in Great Britain
by Amazon